WORLD WAR II
POW CAMPS OF
WYOMING

CHERYL O'BRIEN

THE
History
PRESS

Published by The History Press
Charleston, SC
www.historypress.com

Front cover, top left: Ryan Park German POW timber crew. *Carbon County Museum*; *top center*:
A Fort Warren prisoner of war at work with mop. *Wyoming State Archives*; *top right*: Camp
Clearmont POWs on the Fowler farm. *Photo by Rose Fowler. Sheridan County Museum*; *bottom*:
Prisoner of war camp entrance at unidentified camp. *Photo by U.S. Army Signal Corps, Wyoming
State Archives.*
Back cover: Camp Wheatland POWs working in beet fields in June 1945. *Laramie Peak
Museum, Wheatland, Wyoming, courtesy Judy Wilson*; *inset*: Prisoners of war outside tents at
Camp Douglas. *Wyoming State Archives.*

First published 2019

Manufactured in the United States

ISBN 9781467143820

Library of Congress Control Number: 2019945058

Dedicated to the World War II veterans, including my father, Burton S. Lafin, who served in the U.S. Army Air Forces during World War II.

CONTENTS

PREFACE

My research on Wyoming World War II prisoner of war (POW) camps and prisoners started with an in-depth exploration of Camp Dubois, a World War II German POW timber camp located near my home. I spent a couple of years researching historical documents, military records, old photos and newspaper articles. In addition, I interviewed families of former camp residents and local residents, who shared their memories about the isolated camp and the men who worked there. I wrote an article entitled "Camp Dubois, Wyoming: A Legacy of Literature" that was published in the *Annals of Wyoming: The Wyoming History Journal* in 2015. My research on Camp Dubois continued, and with the help of government officials in Germany, one surviving former Camp Dubois prisoner of war was located and interviewed in 2017 about his experiences in the Wyoming POW camp and other camps he was assigned to. I have shared several of the highlights, photographs and personal stories regarding Camp Dubois U.S. military personnel and POWs to help portray daily life in the camps for the residents.

During my research, I realized how remarkable the history of our Wyoming POW camps and work the prisoners accomplished is, but I also saw how little information has been compiled and documented about this part of our state history. I expanded my research over the past few years to include all Wyoming POW major camps and branch camps, as well as to recognize the base camps from neighboring states that supplied many prisoners to the Wyoming POW camps. I found that there are many people in Wyoming who have valuable information and memories to share about the camps and prisoners. As the years continued to pass, I recognized the immediate need to document the historic records about the POW camps, the stories shared by the camp residents and civilian neighbors and the significance of the World War II POW camps in Wyoming.

My research on Wyoming World War II POW camps and prisoners of war included reviewing historic records and photographs from federal and state agencies; the National and State Archives; state and local museums; the Wyoming National Guard Museum; the American Heritage Center, University of Wyoming; and local libraries, newspapers, private collections, memoirs, correspondence and reviews of other published and unpublished works. In addition, interviews with U.S. military personnel, former prisoners of war, local employers and their families provided further information. Additional details about the former POW camp sites were also obtained from locating, visiting and interpreting the sites and remains.

The combination of these resources helped provide an overview and broad perspective of the operation of Wyoming World War II POW camps and the lives of the camp residents. In addition, the importance of the POW camps and camp labor for Wyoming residents is highlighted. The stories shared by prisoners, U.S. military personnel at the camps and local residents add a personal dimension to the history of Wyoming's POW camps. *World War II POW Camps of Wyoming* shares the story of an important and intriguing part of our state's history.

Note: During World War II, prisoners of war were usually referred to as "PWs" in military reports, newspaper articles and in general conversation. Both "PWs" and "POWs" are used to refer to prisoners of war in this book.

ACKNOWLEDGEMENTS

I would like to acknowledge Lieutenant Harold Harlamert, Camp Dubois commander, for his meticulous record keeping, correspondence and photography that document daily POW camp life and details of the operation of the camps. In addition, I appreciate the information and insight provided by Mr. Kip MacMillan, who related his experience of visiting a POW camp as a young child in an interview I conducted with him several years ago. They helped inspire me to find out more about our Wyoming World War II POW camps and the men who lived and worked in the camps.

I am thankful for the former World War II U.S. military personnel, prisoners of war and the local camp area residents (and their families) who took the time to share their knowledge and experiences. In addition, I appreciate the extent of the efforts by government officials in Germany in locating a surviving former Wyoming POW in 2017 residing in that country who agreed to share his memories of being a prisoner of war. I would also like to acknowledge Bill Sincavage for his assistance and expertise in the compilation of photographs received from many sources and used in this book.

In addition, I would like to acknowledge the staff at the federal and state government agencies, the Wyoming State Museum, the Wyoming State Archives, the Wyoming National Guard Museum, the Warren ICBM and Heritage Museum located at F.E. Warren Air Force Base, the American Heritage Center at the University of Wyoming, the Wyoming Pioneer

Memorial Museum, Camp Douglas Officers' Club State Historic Site, the Legacy of the Plains Museum (Nebraska), as well as local museums, libraries and newspaper offices that showed sincere interest in this research project and provided invaluable information about the POW camps and prisoners of war.

I would especially like to thank my husband, Bill, my research partner, as we traveled throughout Wyoming over the past few years to locate and document the former POW camp sites and information about the prisoners of war and the work they did.

INTRODUCTION

The establishment of Wyoming's World War II prisoner of war (POW) camps resulted in three important major achievements. First, Wyoming's nineteen POW camps, and the other base camps that supplied Wyoming POWs, were operated successfully and adequately provided for the needs of the prisoners of war according to and, in many instances, exceeding Geneva Convention guidelines. Second, the prisoners provided a critically needed labor source, especially for Wyoming's labor-intensive agricultural and timber industries. Third, in spite of the challenges faced by the U.S. military staff who operated the camps, residents and employers who lived in communities that hosted the camps and the prisoners of war who were incarcerated, positive relationships often developed among the groups.

Prisoner of war labor was vital to the success of the maintenance and harvests of agricultural crops and timber operations in Wyoming. The quality of treatment of the prisoners was considered an important factor for the successful development of an organized and productive prisoner of war labor force. Government officials and civilian employers maintained that POWs who were satisfied with their treatment would work harder. In addition, the proper treatment of prisoners in the U.S. POW camps was recognized as an important factor that could potentially influence the treatment received by American prisoners held captive in Axis POW camps.[1]

During and after World War II, approximately 436,000 prisoners of war were held captive in the United States from 1941 into 1946. The prisoners included Germans, Italians, Japanese and those of many other nationalities.[2] The prisoners were housed in 155 large base camps and 511 branch camps across the country.[3]

Wyoming had two major prisoner of war camps and seventeen small branch camps. Camp Douglas served as the major Wyoming base camp that supplied prisoners to many branch camps within the state. The second major Wyoming POW camp operated at Fort Francis E. Warren (Fort Warren), where the prisoners were usually confined to the military base. In addition, many prisoners were sent to Wyoming branch camps for agricultural and timber work from the Scottsbluff, Nebraska POW base camp. POWs were also provided from Camp Greeley, Colorado, in 1944 and 1945.[4]

The operation of the prisoner of war camps was administered primarily by the regional service commands, which operated under the Army Service Forces and Provost Marshal General's Office, in accordance with United States War Department regulations and policies. In 1942, nine service commands were established in the United States. Wyoming was part of the Seventh Service Command, which included nine middle-western states, including Colorado and Nebraska.[5]

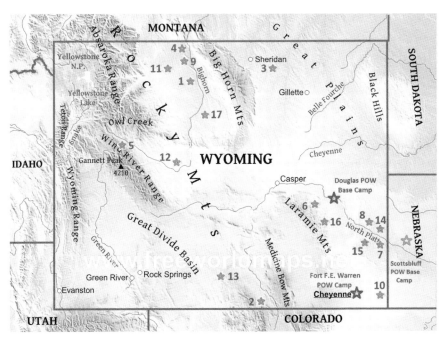

Map showing locations of major POW camps and seventeen branch camps in Wyoming. *Author's map.*

The majority of the prisoners of war were confined in large base camps across the United States that usually accommodated from 2,000 to 4,000 men.[6] Camp Douglas held up to about 3,000 prisoners of war and 5,000 prisoners overall throughout the camp operation.[7] The Fort Francis E. Warren POW camp housed up to approximately 900 prisoners and 3,560 prisoners overall.[8]

The seventeen smaller branch camps in Wyoming were established at locations near where seasonal agricultural and timber labor was needed. Branch camps constructed across the United States usually housed between 250 and 750 prisoners.[9] However, in Wyoming, most of the branch camps housed much smaller groups, between 44 and approximately 400 prisoners.[10]

In Wyoming, there was a particularly critical need for POW labor in the agricultural and timber industries because of manpower shortages due to the war. The majority of the Wyoming branch camps provided labor for agricultural work. Agricultural branch camps operated at Basin, Deaver, Lovell, Powell, Clearmont, Worland, Riverton, Wheatland, Lingle, Torrington, Veteran, Huntley and Pine Bluffs.[11]

In addition, branch camps at Dubois, Esterbrook, Ryan Park, Centennial and a small workforce from Camp Douglas provided labor for the timber industry. Lumbering operations were considered critical to supply needs for construction materials, including crating material for shipping munitions.[12] Many prisoners also cut timber for railroad ties, an important wartime commodity.[13]

PART I

THE PRISONER OF WAR CAMPS

1

POW CAMP OPERATION
AND PRISONER LIFE

ESTABLISHMENT OF POW CAMPS
AND LABOR PROGRAM

In September 1942, the Provost Marshal General's Office developed a prisoner of war camp construction program. The number of incoming POWs to be incarcerated in the United States quickly escalated, which necessitated the immediate need for additional POW housing. Designated areas within existing military bases, former Civilian Conservation Corps (CCC) camps, fairgrounds, auditoriums and tent camps were identified as options to fill critical needs, prior to plans for constructing new facilities.[14]

In Wyoming, the prisoner of war camp at Fort Francis E. Warren utilized a specific area within the existing military base. Six Wyoming prisoner of war camps were established at former CCC camps: Basin, Deaver, Worland, Veteran, Ryan Park and Centennial. Two Wyoming camps utilized armory sites (Camp Lovell and Camp Riverton). Camp Wheatland and Camp Pine Bluffs were constructed at fairground sites. The short-term POW camp at Powell operated at the American Legion building. Other Wyoming POW camps utilized temporary buildings and constructed tent camps. Modifications were made to existing facilities to prepare the camps for the prisoners of war, including installation of perimeter fences, improved lighting (including searchlights) and other security measures.[15]

The first prisoner of war camps were established in Wyoming in 1943 and included Camp Douglas, the Fort Francis E. Warren POW camp and four branch camps at Veteran, Pine Bluffs, Worland and Ryan Park. The Camp Scottsbluff, Nebraska base camp was also in operation in 1943, supplying prisoners to branch camps in Wyoming. In 1944, additional POW branch camps operated in Basin, Deaver, Wheatland, Torrington, Esterbrook and Dubois. In 1945, branch camps were also established at Riverton, Powell, Lovell, Clearmont, Centennial, Lingle and Huntley.[16]

In January 1943, the U.S. government authorized the use of POW labor on military installations. Then, in the fall of 1943, a POW Labor Program was established through the cooperation of the War Department, the War Manpower Commission and the War Food Administration to make prisoner of war labor available to the civilian sector. The Wyoming branch camps were established to provide prisoner labor more efficiently to area farms and local timber operations. Civilian employers worked with local military officials and the Department of Agriculture's Extension Service to obtain prisoner of war labor. The POW Labor Program provided substantial revenue for the U.S. Treasury, which received payment for the difference between the prisoners' daily pay and the standard daily wage after deducting prisoner transportation and other expenses. In June 1945, contractors paid $22 million into the federal treasury for POW labor.[17]

GENEVA CONVENTION GUIDELINES FOR CONSTRUCTION AND OPERATION OF POW CAMPS

The United States strictly followed Geneva Convention guidelines in constructing and operating prisoner of war camps. In general, Wyoming POW camps were constructed to ensure that prisoners were provided with equivalent accommodations as the U.S. Army camp personnel. For example, at many Wyoming camps, both military staff and prisoners were housed in barracks or similar buildings. At other POW camps, both guards and prisoners were housed in tents.[18]

The Geneva Convention specified guidelines regarding the treatment and confinement of prisoners. The daily work schedules of the prisoners could not be excessive, and the prisoners were allowed one day off per week. In Wyoming main camps and branch camps, adherence to these work schedule guidelines was documented and included in military and newspaper reports.[19]

The Geneva Convention also prohibited assigning "unhealthful or dangerous work" to prisoners. Both agricultural and timber work conducted by Wyoming prisoners were recognized as posing normal potential risks. Prisoners were supplied with the same basic protective clothing and equipment as were civilian laborers doing the same work, such as hats, gloves and hard-toed shoes or boots.[20]

Geneva Convention guidelines specified that prisoners who were physically fit could be required to work for their captors. However, officers were exempt from manual labor, and noncommissioned officers were required to do only supervisory work. Officers were entitled to their regular military salaries, even if they didn't work. The prisoners were paid eighty cents per day each day they worked. The money was paid in scrip and could be used at the camp canteen to purchase personal items, snacks, soda and beer or placed in the POW's camp savings account, to be reimbursed when the prisoner was released.[21]

WYOMING PRISONERS OF WAR

During 1943, Italian prisoners of war provided the majority of POW labor at the camps that operated in Wyoming. The Italian prisoners were replaced primarily by German POW labor starting in 1944 following the change in status of many Italian POWs. After Italy surrendered to the Allies in September 1943 and declared war on Germany, Italy became a co-belligerent of the Allies.[22] Italian prisoners who signed a noncombatant agreement could serve in military-related jobs or in the Italian Service Units, which helped to free up U.S. soldiers for combat jobs. The War Department announced that Italian prisoners of war in good standing could work outside of the prison camps without guards, although the new system was to be closely supervised by military officials.[23]

The prisoners of war were a diverse group. In addition to the Italian and German prisoners, there were many other nationalities represented, including Austrian, Czechoslovakian and Polish. Prisoners had individual political beliefs, social customs and religious practices that differed from others. The differences in the prisoners' languages, ages and personalities added to the diversity of the prisoners who were incarcerated together at the POW camps.[24]

Prisoners of war at Camp Douglas. *Wyoming Pioneer Memorial Museum.*

CONFLICTS WITHIN THE CAMPS

Conflicts among the POWs were documented in camp military records. Rivalry sometimes occurred between Italian and German prisoners who were housed at the same camp. For example, at Fort Warren, reports indicate that some German prisoners did not like the Italian prisoners because Italy had changed sides to fight against Germany. In addition, after the Italian prisoners' status changed, they were entitled to camp and work privileges that the German prisoners did not have. There were also conflicts between the German and Austrian prisoners due to their differences in nationality, political beliefs and religion. At the Ryan Park POW camp, many German and Austrian prisoners didn't get along well, and riots between the two groups occurred in the camp. At Camp Veteran, prisoner conflicts reported were associated with strong personalities of some of the prisoners who were at the camp longer than the incoming prisoners.[25]

Prisoners were placed in camps across the Unites States and separated according to Geneva Convention guidelines. The Geneva Convention directed that prisoners of war were to be treated as soldiers. For example, officers were separated from enlisted men, and participation in camp activities between the two groups was segregated. POW officers maintained their authority within the camps. Although the POW officers helped to maintain order, this control, especially by extreme pro-Nazi leaders, often caused internal issues within the camp. Approximately 40 percent of the German prisoners were considered pro-Nazi; 8 to 10 percent were considered extremely pro-Nazi. Problems developed within the camps when the extreme pro-Nazi prisoners actively tried to control the actions and behavior of other camp residents. Some prisoners were targeted and continuously harassed. They were threatened with reprisals if they did not follow pro-Nazi objectives. Killings, assaults and suicides (often forced) were documented in U.S. POW camp military records.[26]

As the War Department became aware of the internal struggles occurring within POW camps, guidelines were established for the identification and segregation of potentially dangerous prisoners. POWs were separated based on knowledge of strong party affiliation. Known pro-Nazi leaders were housed in different sections of the camps or in separate camps from other prisoners. Increased security measures were taken to separate the potentially dangerous prisoners from the general prisoner camp population. In addition, formal procedures were set up at the POW camps for prisoners to voice any concerns they had for their safety.[27]

However, reports of threats by prisoners still occurred, including reports by Wyoming prisoners. Some Wyoming prisoners reported challenges they encountered and incidents of threatening tactics used by pro-Nazi leaders at their assigned camps. At both the Camp Douglas and Camp Scottsbluff base camps, the harassment of prisoners resulted in formal reports of the prisoners' fear for their safety. Some prisoners requested to be relocated to a different camp or took the opportunities to work at the branch camps to get away from the internal camp struggles they faced at the larger base camps.[28]

DAILY LIFE AT WYOMING POW CAMPS

The prisoners at Wyoming's two major camps were housed in barracks at Camp Douglas and in the remodeled stable/garage buildings at Fort Francis E. Warren. The POWs ate in the mess halls and kitchen areas. At Camp Douglas, many prisoners were sent to the smaller branch camps to work on area farms and ranches or in timber operations. At Fort Warren, the prisoners were not sent to other branch camps to work but worked primarily at the military facility.[29]

At the branch camps, work duties varied based on the time of year, specific work assignments and camp conditions. Prisoners were sent to agricultural branch camps primarily during summer and fall months to work on area farms. They worked at irrigating, haying, thinning, hoeing and harvesting crops. Then most prisoners were returned to the base camps. One exception was Camp Veteran, where prisoners remained at the POW camp after crop harvests were completed into the winter months.[30] Prisoners assigned to the timber camps often worked from early summer into the early winter months, until extreme weather and excessive snow depths at the camps stopped work.[31]

The prisoners of war were issued clothing required to be worn while working. Their clothing varied, but many prisoners wore gray or blue denim clothes, usually with large white letters *PW* stenciled on the back of their coats and shirts. In addition, *PW* was often labeled on each sleeve and on the front and back of their pants to clearly identify them as prisoners of war. However, POWs were allowed to wear their own uniforms during their free time. According to a May 1945 article in a local Douglas newspaper, the army reported that many incidents had occurred in which high school students labeled their clothes with *PW*, the prisoner of war identification. Army officials warned against the practice, as students could be mistakenly shot by the military, especially if they failed to halt when ordered.[32]

War prisoners had several options for their free-time activities, especially at the major camps. They played a variety of sports. Many prisoners enjoyed creating art, such as paintings and woodworking items. Some played musical instruments and performed in concerts and plays. In addition, several prisoners wrote poems, essays and journal entries. The POWs had access to camp libraries. Movies were shown at the major camps. Religious services were also provided at the base camps. Many prisoners took a variety of camp courses.[33]

Options for activities and recreation were much more limited at the branch camps. At some branch camps, prisoners still participated in sports, played musical instruments, created artwork, enjoyed woodworking projects, hiked, read and wrote creative literature.[34] Religious services were also provided at several of the branch camps, including the POW camps at Veteran, Worland, Wheatland and Dubois.[35] Some prisoners related that they preferred living at the branch camps and appreciated the close relationships that often developed at the smaller camps.[36]

Prisoners of war stacking hay. *Arnold Krammer Photographic Collection, Legacy of the Plains Museum, Nebraska.*

Prisoners sent postcards and letters to their friends and family postage free through the U.S. Post Office Department. Army censors screened prisoner of war mail to keep track of political issues within the POW camps and to monitor potentially militant POWs. Most Wyoming POW camps accommodated prisoner of war mail correspondence; however, one prisoner reported that POW mail was not allowed to be sent from Camp Veteran while he was a prisoner there.[37]

Even though the prisoners were well fed and taken care of, they still lived as prisoners of war in the camps. They were confined under the control of the U.S. military personnel who operated the camps. The prisoners had to cope with the future uncertainties of their lives. They expressed their intense feelings of homesickness and boredom. In addition, they worried about the welfare of their families and the political conditions in their war-torn home countries.[38]

THE REEDUCATION PROGRAM

A reeducation program for prisoners of war in the United States, named the Intellectual Diversion Program, was initiated on September 6, 1944, by the War Department under the control of the Provost Marshal General's Office. The objective of the program was to teach the prisoners about the democratic form and philosophy of government. Although classes had been offered at the POW base camps soon after they were established, the reeducation program started procedures to assume control over the scope and content of the classes and information provided to the prisoners. The reeducation program operated in secrecy until it was officially announced to the general public on May 28, 1945.[39]

As part of the reeducation program, a national prisoner of war newspaper was created, *Der Ruf* ("The Call"), with input from a select working group of German prisoners. *Der Ruf* was a publication designed to appeal to the more intellectual segment of the prisoner population. The first issue was distributed on March 6, 1945. In addition, extensive review and censorship of camp literature and films were conducted. Approved reading material was substituted, such as literary classics and publications about U.S. geography, natural resources, government, schools, history and institutions. Movies were selected to showcase famous "American statesmen, inventors, military strength and technical achievements." The mandatory viewing by prisoners of "atrocity films" showing the conditions of the concentration camps was imposed.[40]

The reeducation program was conducted at the major prisoner of war camps in Wyoming, Camp Douglas and Fort Francis E. Warren. At the Fort Warren POW camp, an extensive variety of courses was provided. The reeducation program at Camp Douglas was more limited in the scope of courses but included the standard classes in democratic government and English. U.S. Army staff at Camp Douglas reported that "the good guys responded well" to the rigorous educational program. However, many prisoners were not receptive to what they considered to be American propaganda. Pro-Nazi camp leaders actively renounced U.S. reeducation program objectives.[41]

The success of the reeducation program was difficult to assess, in part because it was offered to only a specific prisoner population recognized as the most likely group for the program to be well received. The content of the program was extremely condensed and was presented over a short period of time. In addition, there was a very limited number of adequate follow-up surveys of former prisoners to accurately determine the program's influence and outcome. According to Arnold Krammer, the reeducation program was considered "a reasonable success," in spite of "the shortcomings caused by secrecy and haste."[42]

POW CAMP MILITARY RECORDS

The number of POWs present in specific camps in Wyoming fluctuated as the war progressed. Prisoner of war labor provided to branch camps was contingent on the availability of prisoner labor, conditions within the camps, the seasonal nature of the work required and the priority of labor needs. Prisoner of War Camp Labor Reports were completed by the POW camp commander twice a month for each camp that documented details of prisoner populations, work performed in man-days and additional comments, such as camp setup and closure dates.[43]

Prisoners of war were processed and assigned serial numbers used for identification in holding areas near combat areas where they were captured or when they arrived in the United States. This identification number was important to accurately document, identify and track the prisoners throughout their internment in the United States. When prisoners were assigned serial numbers near their capture area, the numbers had two parts. The first part included a number that identified the theater in which the prisoner was captured. (For example, North Africa was designated as 81 and Europe was 31.) In addition, a letter identifying the prisoner's country of service followed this number, such as *G* for Germany or *I* for Italy. The second part of the serial number was a consecutive number assigned to the specific prisoner.[44]

However, if the prisoner wasn't assigned a serial number until he arrived in the United States, the first part of the serial number included the number of the Army Service Command (1–9) in which he was assigned. For example, Wyoming was located within the Seventh Service Command. Then a *W* for War Department followed. Next was the first letter that identified the prisoner's country of service. Last, a consecutive number was assigned to the prisoner.[45]

Each prisoner completed a form that included his serial number, medical history, fingerprints and capture information. This form served as the prisoner's permanent record as an official prisoner of war. Copies were

WAR DEPARTMENT OFFICE OF THE PROVOST MARSHAL GENERAL **PRISONER OF WAR CAMP LABOR REPORT**			Reports Control Symbol MGA 48 (R±) PMG OFFICE USE ONLY

	R	1
	E	2
	C	3

CAMP	PERIOD ENDING
P.O.W. Branch Camp NO. 8, Dubois, Wyoming.	15 January 1946

BASE CAMP	NATIONALITY
P.O.W. Camp, Scottsbluff, Nebraska.	German

Part I. TOTAL MAN-DAYS AND LABOR AVAILABILITY

1. TOTAL MAN-DAYS OF ALL PRISONERS IN THIS CAMP DURING THIS PERIOD:	OFFICERS	NCO'S	PRIVATES	TOTAL
		15	465	480

NONWORKERS		WORKERS	
2. REASON FOR NONWORKER STATUS:		3. WORK ASSIGNMENT STATUS:	
(a) PHYSICALLY UNABLE TO WORK	2	(a) WORKED	304
(b) TEMPORARY MEDICAL REASONS		(b) ASSIGNED, DID NOT WORK	110
(c) DISCIPLINARY ACTION		(c) NOT ASSIGNED TO WORK	
(d) NONWORKING OFFICERS		TOTAL, WORKED OR AVAILABLE	414
(e) NONWORKING NCO'S		4. REST DAYS OF WORKERS	64
(f) OTHER REASONS (explain)			
TOTAL MAN-DAYS, NONWORKERS	2	TOTAL MAN-DAYS, WORKERS	478

Part II. MAN-DAYS WORKED, BY PROJECTS

PROJECT CODE	SHORT TITLE	TOTAL MAN-DAYS	PROJECT CODE	SHORT TITLE	TOTAL MAN-DAYS
	PW CAMP OVERHEAD			**CONTRACT WORK**	
10	COMPANY AND STOCKADE, UNPAID		51	AGRICULTURE	
11	COMPANY AND STOCKADE, PAID	42	52	PULPWOOD, LOGS, AND LUMBER	241
12	PW CANTEEN		53	MINING AND QUARRYING	
13	PW OFFICERS' ORDERLIES, COOKS		54	CONSTRUCTION	
14	PW MEDICAL	12	55	FOOD PROCESSING	
15	CAMP HEADQUARTERS		56	OTHER MANUFACTURING	
16	CAMP PW FUND		57	TRANSPORTATION	
19	OTHER PW CAMP (explain)		58	TRADE	
	SUBTOTAL	54	59	OTHER NONGOVERNMENTAL	
	SERVICE COMMAND ACTIVITIES		60	PUBLIC CONTRACT (explain)	
				SUBTOTAL	241
21	SVC POST CONTRACT WORK			**NAVY WORK**	
22	SVC ACTIVITIES, THIS POST	9			
23	SVC ACTIVITIES, OTHER POSTS:		71		
	SUBTOTAL	9			
	TECHNICAL SERVICES ACTIVITIES			**RECAPITULATION**	
				PW CAMP OVERHEAD	54
				SERVICE COMMAND ACTIVITIES	9
				TECHNICAL SERVICES ACTIVITIES	
				ARMY AIR FORCES ACTIVITIES	
				CONTRACT WORK	241
	SUBTOTAL			NAVY WORK	
	ARMY AIR FORCES ACTIVITIES			TOTAL	304
41				* Must equal Part I, Item 3a.	

WD AGO FORM 19-21 Replaces WD PMG Form 27, rev., and WD AGO 19-21 (1 Apr 1945), which are obsolete. 1 JUL 1944   10—45110-1

Prisoners of War Camp Labor Report, Dubois, Wyoming, January 15, 1946. *U.S. War Department, National Archives.*

provided to the International Red Cross and Swiss authorities, who were responsible for notifying the prisoner's family that he was a prisoner of war.[46]

Wyoming camp prisoner of war rosters that include the POW serial numbers were valuable for analyzing details pertaining to prisoners' nationality, capture information and group diversity. The number and names of the prisoners assigned to specific camps often changed as work

1.	1 Alfter	Heinrich	81G-230884
2.	165 Bareth	Alois	7WG-34388
3.	41 Benesch	Rudolf	81G-230992
4.	5 Bichler	Franz	81G-231279
5.	6 Born	Nikolaus	81G-230807
6.	142 Burkhardt	Otto	7WG-65680
7.	82 Clausius	Hans	7WG-28077
8.	166 Forster	Michael	81G-230117
9.	167 Franz	Konrad	7WG-44872
10.	127 Friedl	Wilhelm	81G-231292
11.	148 Gerdes	Peter	7WG-65802
12.	168 Glodek	Rudolf	7WG-21582
13.	Goebel	Heinz	7WG-37152
14.	48 Hiemer	Rolf	81G-231238
15.	130 Innreiter	Friedrich	81G-231188
16.	169 Kay	Arthur	7WG-21660
17.	18 Koch	Heinrich	81G-231240
18.	154 Koenicke	Guenther	7WG-65055
19.	159 Reinz	Helmut	7WG-65389
20.	29 Schmitz	Johann	81G-230943
21.	171 Schulz	Alfred	31G-140447
22.	61 Schweppe	Guenther	81G-231155
23.	35 Steber	Walter	81G-230843
24.	36 Tausch	Ernst	81G-231153
25.	174 Triebess	Wolfgang	31G-140186
26.	163 Weikl	Friedrich	7WG-66437
27.	73 Wilhelm	Heinrich	7WG-28099
28.	179 Wucharz	Erwin	31G-140276
29.	45 Cordes	Georg	81G-231156
30.	178 Wilkowski	Paul	31G-140190

nov. 14, 1944

I hereby acknowledge receipt of the above listed thirty men from P.O.W. Branch Camp no. 7, Dubois, Wyoming.

Harry Petchy
1st Sgt

Roster of POWs being transferred from Camp Dubois. *Harold Harlamert Camp Dubois Records, 1944–1946, courtesy Linda Siemens.*

needs changed, along with the overall makeup of camp residents. For example, review of a roster of thirty POWs from Camp Dubois being transferred back to the base camp in November 1944 reveals that all prisoners were German, fourteen captured in North Africa and four captured in the European campaign. In addition, twelve prisoners were processed after they arrived in the United States; they were assigned to the Seventh Service Command.[47]

In addition, prisoner of war serial numbers were helpful in tracking information about the former prisoners after the war ended. In 2016, as part of the research on Wyoming World War II POW camps, a camp roster was sent to government officials in Germany to attempt to locate surviving former POWs. In 2017, German government officials were able to locate one surviving former prisoner of war using the roster of names and serial numbers provided. The former Wyoming prisoner of war provided valuable information about prisoner daily life and a firsthand account of his experiences in Wyoming POW camps.[48]

CAMP SECURITY MEASURES

Security measures at the POW camps were taken very seriously, particularly during the initial period of operation of the camps. Strict security was maintained at the camps, including the number of guards assigned to work details outside of the camps. Prisoner escapes and potential sabotage were major concerns of the U.S. government, especially in and nearby the communities where the prisoner of war camps were located.[49]

As the war progressed, the strict security measures in Wyoming agricultural and timber camps and during work details relaxed. The ratio of guards decreased, and more freedom was allowed for the prisoners who worked outside the camps. Former prisoners and area residents reported that the POW camp gates were often left open at some branch camps, especially after the war in Europe ended.[50]

PRISONER ESCAPES AND TEMPORARY ABSENCES

According to Krammer, 2,827 prisoners escaped from prisoner of war camps across the United States between 1942 and 1946. There are no documented records of any assaults on U.S. citizens or sabotage committed by prisoners who escaped from the camps. Most escapees were recaptured within three days; however, one German prisoner of war who escaped in 1945 surrendered forty years later, in 1985.[51]

At least eighteen escapes from Wyoming POW camps are documented. The majority of prisoner escapes were from the major camps at Camp Douglas and Fort Francis E. Warren.[52] In addition, there were a few escapes reported from the branch camps, including the Ryan Park POW camp, Camp Torrington and Camp Wheatland. All the prisoners were recaptured, except one prisoner who was shot and killed during his escape attempt at Camp Douglas. The recaptured prisoners were returned to their camps to face disciplinary action.[53]

The Geneva Convention, Article 45, specifies that prisoners of war are subject to "all laws, regulations and orders" as the military personnel of the detaining army. Therefore, POWs faced the same disciplinary actions. The POW camp commander could choose to discipline prisoners with administrative pressure or disciplinary measures. Prisoners who attempted to escape were often placed in confinement up to thirty days, with the additional option to limit the prisoner to a restricted diet for up to fourteen days. The War Department recommended fourteen days in confinement for the first escape attempt and thirty days for a second escape.[54]

There are also several reports of prisoners being sent from the Wyoming POW camps to run errands. In addition, some prisoners left their camps on their own to visit other people or establishments. The prisoners who were temporarily absent from the POW camps returned voluntarily. When the prisoners snuck in and out of the POW camps, reports indicate that they climbed over or went under the camp fences.[55]

WYOMING PRISONER OF WAR DEATHS

Prisoner deaths occurred in Wyoming POW camps, at work sites and in area hospitals. The majority of deaths involved prisoners at the major camps. Some prisoners died outside of Wyoming (for example, at out-of-state hospitals) but were buried at the major camp cemeteries. At Fort Francis E. Warren, nine prisoners are buried, including eight German prisoners and one Italian prisoner.[56] At Camp Douglas, six POW deaths were documented, including four German prisoners and two Italians. The prisoners were temporarily buried at Camp Douglas and transferred to Fort Riley, Kansas National Cemetery for final burial.[57]

Deaths also occurred at the POW branch camp work sites. A German prisoner was killed near the Ryan Park POW camp by a falling tree in November 1944.[58] In August 1945, another German POW died when a tree he cut fell on him during a strong wind gust near Camp Dubois.[59] A Camp Veteran prisoner was also killed in August 1945. The POW was hauling barley in a farm truck and misjudged an approach bridge over an irrigation canal. The truck overturned and crashed into the canal, where the prisoner drowned. In November 1945, two additional POWs from Camp Veteran were killed and several prisoners injured when a truck they were riding in rolled over.[60]

2

MAJOR POW CAMPS IN WYOMING

CAMP DOUGLAS, CONVERSE COUNTY

Camp Douglas Serves as Major POW Base Camp

Camp Douglas operated as the major prisoner of war base camp in Wyoming from August 1943 to February 1946, providing prisoners to many Wyoming branch camps. The POW camp was designed to accommodate up to approximately three thousand prisoners of war.[61] In addition, over five hundred military personnel, including enlisted men and about fifty officers, were stationed at the camp. A total of approximately two thousand Italian and three thousand German prisoners of war were housed at Camp Douglas overall.[62]

The Douglas POW camp was located about one mile west of Douglas. The camp site extended over a square mile. The camp construction cost was approximately $2 million and included 180 buildings. The complex included a modern hospital to accommodate 150 patients. The camp had its own internal road system and fire department. In addition, water, sewer and electrical systems were installed.[63]

The U.S. military personnel and prisoners were housed in barracks that accommodated up to fifty men. The POWs were divided among three separate fenced compounds. The prisoners ran their own bakery and barber, shoe, tailor and carpenter shops.[64]

On June 15, 1943, a "Grand Opening" was held for the public to tour the new Douglas Prisoner of War Camp. Approximately two thousand people from across Wyoming toured the site. A local newspaper reported that the public was impressed by the use of the latest equipment available at the camp.[65]

In August 1943, a local corporation, Converse Labor Inc., was formed to help facilitate prisoner of war labor needs. Membership was open to all area farmers and ranchers needing prisoner labor.[66] A contract between the War Department and Converse Labor was signed in late August to help relieve local manpower shortages, primarily for agricultural work.[67]

U.S. Army Douglas Prisoner of War Camp sign. *Wyoming State Archives.*

Camp Residents Arrive

The first group of military police, who served as guards at Camp Douglas, arrived by train on August 9, 1943. Many Douglas residents lined the streets to watch them march across the river to the new POW camp. A local newspaper reported that they were a "snappy company, fully equipped with pack, gun, and helmet," and they marched "with a rhythmic step and eyes straight ahead."[68]

On August 13, 1943, the first group of 412 prisoners of war arrived. The prisoners were Italians who were captured in Tunisia. A large crowd gathered at the train station to watch as the prisoners were escorted by guards to the prisoner of war camp. At the camp, the prisoners were assigned to their quarters and issued new clothing. Medical attention at the camp hospital was immediately provided to ten of the prisoners suffering from wounds and illnesses. Camp officials reported that, in general, the prisoners appeared well cared for and were well trained.[69]

Camp Douglas Prisoner of War Labor

Camp Douglas operated under strict compliance with Geneva Convention rules that specified guidelines for the use and conditions of prisoner of war labor. In late September 1943, prisoners became available to work on area farms and ranches. The prisoners were closely guarded. They were picked up daily from the camp at 7:30 a.m., transported to area farms to work and returned to the camp by 6:00 p.m., except on Sundays. Prisoners could work up to nine hours a day, but guidelines stipulated that they not spend more than ten hours away from the POW camp.[70]

By the end of September 1943, there were approximately 1,900 Italian prisoners of war at Camp Douglas. The prisoners included enlisted men and 27 officers. They had been captured primarily in North Africa and Sicily.[71]

During the fall of 1943, Camp Douglas provided prisoner labor for harvesting beets, potatoes and other crops in the Worland, Wheatland and Douglas areas. In addition, Camp Douglas supplied prisoners to work in the Greeley and Gilcrest, Colorado areas. In November 1943, a Holly Sugar Company representative reported in the local newspaper that the area beet harvest was nearly completed and that the "prisoner labor saved the day for the beet harvest."[72]

Prisoners of war outside tents at Camp Douglas. *Wyoming State Archives*.

In addition to agricultural labor provided in 1943, some prisoners worked for the timber industry. A work crew of about fifty Camp Douglas prisoners was assigned to cutting down timber west of Casper. Approximately 150 Italian prisoners from Camp Douglas were sent for training on how to properly cut timber at the Ryan Park POW camp near Saratoga.[73]

As the status of the Italian prisoners changed, most were soon replaced by German prisoners. In April 1944, a local newspaper announced that about thirty German prisoners of war started working at local ranches. Reports from area farmers and ranchers indicated that the German prisoners were "faster, more competent than the former Italian laborers." It was anticipated that more German POW labor would be available to farmers and ranchers as the need for help increased.[74]

Camp Douglas was temporarily deactivated on July 15, 1944. Local citizens appealed to government officials to reopen the POW camp. According to the commanding general of the Seventh Service Command, the decision to temporarily close the camp was based on "economy in personnel" and costs. However, Camp Douglas was reactivated approximately two weeks later, on August 3, 1944.[75] On September 19, 1944, a group of 471 German prisoners of war arrived at the camp. The incoming prisoners had been captured during the initial stages of the invasion of France.[76]

Camp Douglas Prisoner Conflicts

The German prisoners included a group of die-hard "Nazi and SS officers." This group worked diligently to create unrest and difficulties for the prisoners who followed the POW camp rules and directives. The extreme pro-Nazi soldiers were isolated in separate compounds.[77]

However, the pro-Nazi prisoners continuously harassed and sometimes attacked targeted prisoners from other compounds. Camp officials reported that some pro-Nazi extremists left their compound at night and snuck into other compounds to assault other prisoners. These attacks caused some prisoners to fear for their lives.[78]

In October 1944, Viktor Fuchs, a German noncommissioned officer, was reported missing. At first, camp officials believed he had escaped. However, he was later found hiding in the attic of an old camp building. It was believed that Fuchs had been hiding from the pro-Nazi soldiers. In November 1944, additional camp security measures were taken. Double fences were installed around the prisoner compounds, and guard dogs were assigned to patrol the area.[79]

Fencing installed around prisoner compounds at Camp Douglas. *Wyoming State Archives*.

Douglas POW Camp Life

The prisoners enjoyed playing sports and were provided with recreation equipment. Soccer was a favorite sport. On Sunday afternoons, intercompany games were organized. In addition, prisoners were allowed to take hikes accompanied by camp guards. The prisoners listened to radios that were donated by welfare agencies. They also published camp newspapers. The POWs visited with one another at their separate compounds. They were also allowed to visit with relatives and friends at specified times within the stockade. Movies were shown several times a week. Prisoners could purchase candy, cigarettes and soda at the canteens located in each compound.[80]

Prisoners created a variety of artwork, including paintings and sketches. Italian prisoners painted seventeen murals on the walls of the U. S. Officers' Club that featured Western-themed scenes, including cowboys roping horses, a barroom scene and landscapes.[81] A few of the prisoners even made clocks and violins. In addition, the prisoners carved wooden items, including bowls, boxes and sculptures.[82]

Cesare Oriano was an Italian prisoner of war who was incarcerated at Camp Douglas in May or June 1943. He worked as a cook at the camp.

Left: Wood carving of tank made by a German POW and given to a camp guard. *Photo by Richard Collier, Wyoming Department of State Parks and Cultural Resources. Wyoming Pioneer Memorial Museum.*

Right: Wood carving of an airplane by a POW who was believed to be a pilot for the Luftwaffe. *Photo by Richard Collier, Wyoming Department of State Parks and Cultural Resources. Wyoming Pioneer Memorial Museum.*

Oriano said that the prisoners were treated very well at the Douglas POW camp. He related how the POWs used scrap wood to build a Catholic church and theater. Oriano reported that he was the only Italian prisoner who returned to Wyoming to live after the war, although other Italian POWs returned to the United States to live in other states.[83]

Prisoner Escapes and Deaths at Camp Douglas

The army followed strict security measures at Camp Douglas. In addition to the two Police Escort Guard companies who guarded the prisoners, German Shepherds patrolled the inner stockade fence twenty-four hours a day. In spite of the security precautions, there were several documented escape attempts from Camp Douglas.[84]

One prisoner was shot and killed during his escape attempt by a guard posted in the guard tower. Six other prisoners who escaped from Camp Douglas were all recaptured. In April 1945, two prisoners escaped and were recaptured three days later downriver in a haystack wearing six pairs of "GI winter underwear" to keep them warm.[85] In addition, three German prisoners escaped from the camp on May 1, 1945.[86] The escape was well planned and showed evidence of prisoner ingenuity and teamwork. The escapees were assisted by other prisoners assigned to a garbage detail. They hid the prisoners in large garbage cans that were transported out of the camp by horses. The prisoners were set free near the North Platte River. Back at the POW camp, fellow prisoners made dummies to represent the escaped prisoners at roll call. They held up the dummies and spoke for the missing prisoners. The camp officer realized and confirmed the ruse when he grabbed the arm of one of the dummies. A search was conducted, and the prisoners were recaptured three days later.[87]

In addition to the prisoner who was killed while attempting to escape, other deaths occurred at Camp Douglas. Six Italian and German prisoners were temporarily buried at the POW camp cemetery before being transferred to Fort Riley, Kansas National Cemetery for final burial in January 1946. Some prisoners died from war injuries and medical issues they suffered prior to coming to Camp Douglas, such as a fourteen-year-old soldier who died from gangrene due to untreated battle wounds.[88] Not all the prisoners who were buried in the camp cemetery died at Camp Douglas. For example, POW Captain Giacome

Greco died in a Denver hospital in March 1944 and was buried at the Camp Douglas cemetery. A full military funeral was conducted for Greco. An Italian flag was placed over his coffin. Music for the service was provided by Italian singers from the camp.[89]

Camp Douglas Closes and Is Dismantled

The population of prisoners at Camp Douglas peaked at 3,011 men in the summer of 1945.[90] The prisoners continued to work at Camp Douglas and from the branch camps through the fall of 1945 and into early winter of 1945–46. Plans for repatriation were developed by the U.S. military and Camp Douglas officials, including the logistics of providing transportation for the prisoners from Wyoming back to Europe.[91]

The majority of prisoners were shipped out from Camp Douglas starting in early January 1946. By January 24, only a small group of 130 "trusted" prisoners remained with a few guards. Camp officials reported that the camp would be deactivated in early February 1946.[92]

After Camp Douglas closed, the property was sold to Converse County for one dollar.[93] Plans for transferring ownership, moving camp buildings and the dismantling of the buildings were made. In July 1946, the U.S. Employment Service advertised for local carpenters and laborers to sign up to work on the removal of the buildings. Lumber and other building materials from the dismantled buildings at the former POW camp were to be sold exclusively for the construction of housing for veterans.[94] The hospital facilities were transferred to Converse County in early September 1946.[95]

Camp Douglas was dismantled "in the record time of sixty days." Evidence of the existence of the former POW camp continued to quickly disappear. Workers found many murals and sketches created by the prisoners on interior walls of buildings. They also found lamp shades, furniture and irons made by the prisoners from scraps of materials.[96] Another reminder of the prisoners who were housed at the camp surfaced when an area contractor found a German pistol, holster and ammunition hidden in the walls of a camp building he was dismantling.[97]

The former Camp Douglas Officers' Club is the only original building that still stands on the former POW camp site. The Officers' Club building had several owners after Camp Douglas closed. It was purchased by the Douglas Lodge No. 15, Independent Order of Odd Fellows, in 1963.

g.   Officers' Club

Above: Murals and a pool table are part of the décor in the Officers' Club at Camp Douglas. *Photo by Richard Collier, Wyoming Department of State Parks and Cultural Resources. Wyoming Pioneer Memorial Museum.*

Opposite, top: A German pistol with holster and ammunition was found during demolition in building walls at Camp Douglas. *Courtesy Richard Fink.*

Opposite, bottom: The Camp Douglas Officers' Club features murals painted by Italian POWs and is a State Historic Site. *Wyoming Pioneer Memorial Museum.*

The Camp Douglas Officers' Club was designated a State Historic Site in 2012 and is administered by the Wyoming Department of State Parks and Cultural Resources. The murals painted on the walls of the officers' club by the Italian prisoners and other Camp Douglas photos and artifacts are on display at the site. In addition, the Wyoming Pioneer Memorial Museum, located near the former POW camp site, contains historic records and original artifacts relating to Camp Douglas.[98]

FORT FRANCIS E. WARREN POW CAMP, LARAMIE COUNTY

Fort Francis E. Warren (Fort Warren) POW Camp Operates from 1943 into 1946

A prisoner of war camp operated at the Fort Francis E. Warren military post in Cheyenne (now F.E. Warren Air Force Base) from early February 1943 into late April 1946. The prisoners were primarily kept at the post.[99] The POW camp housed more than 900 prisoners at a time, with a total of over 3,560 Italian and German prisoners of war during its operation.[100] A high fence topped with barbed wire enclosed the barracks. Military police and trained dogs guarded the camp.[101]

Fort Warren Prisoners of War

Information about the prisoners was censored by the army, so public details about the prisoners, their accommodations and the work they did was extremely limited. Prisoners did maintenance work, such as cleaning, painting, mowing and carpentry. Other POWs worked in the hospital laboratory, kitchens, laundry and as gardeners.[102]

The first group of Italian prisoners arrived at the Fort Francis E. Warren POW camp on February 1, 1943. On November 13, 1943, a group of 350 German prisoners of war was sent to the camp. Many of the prisoners at Fort Warren had served in the Afrika Korps and suffered from poor health and illnesses, so a Prisoner of War Patient Detachment was also established.[103]

German prisoners shared the POW camp with Italian prisoners, but the two groups were separated from each other because of strong political differences. The German prisoners were housed within a fenced compound. After the status of the Italian prisoners changed in September 1943, most Italian POWs signed noncombatant agreements. Many Italian prisoners of war worked at Fort Warren and served in the Italian Service Units. The Italian prisoners were housed in army barracks. In May 1944, Italian POWs received noncombat training at Fort Warren.[104]

Italian POW Cesare Oriano provided detailed information about the Fort Warren POW camp. According to Oriano, both he and his brother were sent to Fort Warren in November 1943 as members of Italian Service Units. They were allowed visitors once a week. Italian Americans came to visit

Right: A Fort Warren prisoner of war at work with mop. *Wyoming State Archives*.

Below: Fort Warren German POWs taking a break from their work. *Wyoming State Archives*.

the Italian POWs at Fort Warren to show their hospitality to the homesick soldiers. Oriano met his future wife during one of the camp visits. He reported that the Italian prisoners were treated with respect and humanity, both as POWs and as members of the Italian Service Units. After the war, Oriano returned to Cheyenne, Wyoming, where he married, raised a family and worked as a respected businessman.[105]

Prisoner Accommodations at the Fort Warren POW Camp

Prisoners were housed in two barracks that had previously served as stables and garage buildings. The barracks, constructed in 1911, were approximately two hundred feet long by seventy feet wide. They were designed to house approximately 106 animals each. The barracks had brick walls, brick and clay floors, a concrete foundation and slate roofs. The buildings were equipped with electricity and water and sewer systems. The POW camp area was fenced, and there was an exercise area between the two barracks buildings. Renovations to the barracks to upgrade living conditions for the prisoners were made in April 1945. The remodeling included a new steam heating system, bathroom facilities and additional windows to provide better ventilation and lighting to comply with Geneva Convention guidelines.[106]

Fort Warren POW camp barracks previously used as stables and a garage. *Warren ICBM and Heritage Museum at F.E. Warren Air Force Base.*

A Headquarters Office for the POW camp commanding officer was located outside of the fenced area. In addition, a two-story Administration Building was utilized by prisoners. The Administration Building included a meeting area where business was conducted and assignments were made. There were also dayrooms and an area for the prisoners to eat. The former barracks, Headquarters Office and Administration Building remain in use today on the military base.[107]

POW Camp Activities

The prisoners took part in camp sports and recreation, including soccer, handball and table tennis. They enjoyed entertainment such as plays and concerts. The prisoners were provided with musical instruments and assembled a camp orchestra. Religious services were conducted on a regular basis at the Fort Warren POW camp. The prisoners also liked to paint, draw and craft items from materials discarded by others.[108]

The prisoners were also provided with the opportunity to attend camp school, which included a wide range of courses. In February 1945, reports specified that 241 prisoners were enrolled in classes that included German, English, history, geography, electronics, industrial management, heavy equipment operation and accounting. A formal reeducation program was eventually established that included providing the prisoners with information relating to reeducation objectives in the camp newspaper and magazine. The camp newspaper, *Der Zaungast* ("The Fence Guest"), was distributed weekly from April 1944 to May 1945. It contained articles translated from newspapers, such as the *New York Times*, with a special focus on events occurring in Germany. Camp announcements, prisoner literature, sports reports and puzzles were also included.[109]

Fort Warren POW painting purchased by a former F.E. Warren Air Force officer at a local garage sale who noticed the POW signature. *Photo by Paula Taylor, Warren ICBM and Heritage Museum.*

The magazine, *Lagermagazin* ("Camp Magazine"), was distributed twice a month from August 1945 through January 1946 and focused on information pertaining to U.S. Army reeducation goals. World news, educational articles, literary works and sports reports were included. In addition, discussions of political and social issues and upcoming challenges to be faced in Europe's war-torn countries were featured.[110]

Prisoner Escape Attempts

There are reports of a few unsuccessful escape attempts from the Fort Francis E. Warren POW camp. In June 1944, two escaped German prisoners were recaptured almost three miles from the camp by a Fort Warren army captain who was with American troops on maneuvers in the Pole Mountain area. The captain was driving along the highway west of Cheyenne when he saw and recognized the men as escaped prisoners of war. The prisoners were taken into custody and returned to the Fort Warren POW camp, where camp officials were not yet aware the prisoners had escaped. The prisoners had made their escape by jumping aboard a freight train passing nearby. Another escaped Fort Warren prisoner was recaptured in a Denver theater lobby on August 10, 1944.[111]

Fort Francis E. Warren POW Cemetery

A POW cemetery was established adjacent to the Fort Francis E. Warren Post Cemetery within a separate enclosed fenced area. It is the only remaining World War II POW cemetery in Wyoming. Nine prisoners of war—one Italian and eight German prisoners—are buried there.[112] Records indicate that at least two of the prisoners died in Colorado but were buried at Fort Warren. All of the prisoners died of natural causes, except one German prisoner who committed suicide on May 6, 1945, after finding out that Adolf Hitler had died. The cemetery is well maintained.[113] The German embassy still sends money to place flowers on the graves on special occasions, such as German Memorial Day, which is celebrated in November.[114]

Fort Warren POW Camp Closes

The Fort Francis E. Warren Prisoner of War Camp was deactivated on April 27, 1946. An exhibit about the Fort Warren camp and the prisoners of war is on display at the Warren ICBM and Heritage Museum. A painting by a former prisoner of war, prisoner clothing found in the rafters of the former barracks and photos are among the artifacts included in the exhibit.[115]

Above: Fort Warren POW cemetery located adjacent to the base cemetery. *Author's collection.*

Left: Fort Warren PW long johns found in the rafters of one of the barracks. *Photo by Paula Taylor, Warren ICBM and Heritage Museum.*

3

CAMP SCOTTSBLUFF, NEBRASKA POW BASE CAMP

CAMP SCOTTSBLUFF PROVIDES PRISONERS TO WYOMING POW CAMPS

Although Camp Scottsbluff was located in Nebraska, it served as a major base camp that provided prisoners of war to many Wyoming branch camps. Camp Scottsbluff operated from June 1943 into March 1946 under the U.S. War Department, Seventh Service Command. Prisoners were supplied from base camps to branch camps located across state lines within the Seventh Service Command region.[116]

THE POW CAMP AT SCOTTSBLUFF

Camp Scottsbluff was built to house up to five thousand prisoners and the military staff needed to operate the camp. The camp was designed following the standard layout for a POW camp of five thousand prisoners.[117] It consisted of three separate compounds and included wood-frame barracks that each held fifty men. The camp was self-contained, with its own water and sewer systems. Cooking and shower facilities were provided for the prisoners. The POW camp also included officer quarters, a mess hall, a hospital, a garrison area and a well house. The structures were enclosed within a double fence of barbed wire with guard towers overlooking the compounds.[118]

Scottsbluff POW camp photo taken from helicopter. *Fairfield Photographic Collection, Legacy of Plains Museum.*

CAMP SCOTTSBLUFF PRISONER LABOR

Prisoners were sent to nearby branch camps for specific work assignments that primarily supported the agricultural and timber industries. Several hundred Italian prisoners first arrived in Camp Scottsbluff in June 1943. In late July, a local newspaper announced that prisoners would be available to work on area farms. Local County Extension Agents and farmers followed War Department regulations specific to the use of prisoner of war labor. Branch camps were soon established near farm and timber communities to better supply labor needs.[119]

In late September 1943, an area newspaper reported that Italian prisoners were aiding in the labor shortage. Specific details for acquiring prisoner of war labor were listed. Farmers had to contract as a group to obtain prisoner labor. The State Extension Service needed to approve their application, and the War Department had to certify the need for the emergency labor requested. The cost for prisoner labor was the same as the cost for civilian labor. Contracts specified assistance with the sugar beet, potato and bean harvests. In addition, some additional irrigation ditch and general farmwork was approved.[120]

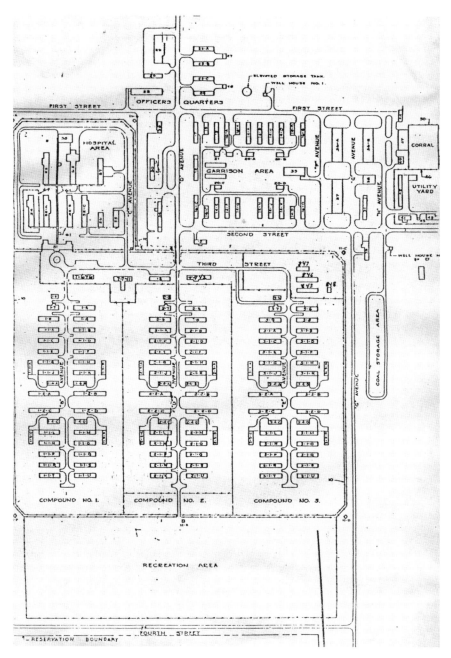

Scottsbluff POW camp site map showing prisoner compounds and recreation area. *Legacy of the Plains Museum.*

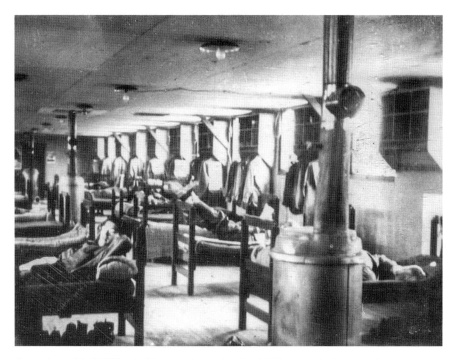

Camp Scottsbluff POWs inside camp barracks. *Fairfield Photographic Collection, Legacy of the Plains Museum.*

CAMP LIFE

The Camp Scottsbluff prisoners enjoyed sports and recreation in their spare time. They played volleyball, soccer, handball and Ping-Pong. The Italian prisoners especially liked to play bocce. The prisoners also enjoyed painting, crafts and woodworking projects. Many prisoners utilized the POW camp library. In addition, a camp band and an orchestra were formed. Camp Scottsbluff prisoners also enjoyed movies, especially musicals and Westerns. In July 1944, approximately 950 prisoners registered for camp courses. A variety of courses were offered, including English, German and French language classes.[121]

CAMP CHALLENGES AND CONFLICTS

After the Italian prisoners' status changed in September 1943, German prisoners replaced many Italian prisoners assigned to fill other specific jobs

Camp Scottsbluff Italian POWs playing bocce during their free time. Note the guard tower in the background. *Fairfield Photographic Collection, Legacy of the Plains Museum.*

contributing to the war effort. Many of the first German prisoners who came to Camp Scottsbluff had served in General Erwin Rommel's Afrika Korps and were captured in North Africa. In addition to the German soldiers, the prisoners included soldiers from countries that Germany had conquered, including Austria, Poland, Czechoslovakia and Yugoslavia.[122]

The prisoners in Camp Scottsbluff represented men with a variety of nationalities, languages and political views, which often caused challenges and conflicts among the men. Camp military records include many requests from prisoners who felt threatened by pro-Nazi radicals to be relocated to other camps.[123] In 1944, one former Camp Dubois POW, Rudolf Ritschel, reported serious personal safety concerns to American camp officials. Ritschel related that conditions within the Scottsbluff POW camp became more threatening as the news of defeats of the German troops increased. He and six other prisoners requested a transfer from the Scottsbluff POW camp to another camp to distance themselves from other prisoners in the camp.[124]

Another report documents that a Camp Scottsbluff prisoner was severely beaten by other camp prisoners for writing a letter to his father, who was an American resident. The pro-Nazi prisoners warned him not to write the letter, because his father was "not a good Nazi." The POW did not listen to them and ended up in the hospital for treatment of his injuries. The report indicates that the incident was not witnessed by American military personnel stationed at the camp.[125]

A DARING CROSS-COUNTRY ESCAPE

On July 11, 1944, two German prisoners, Karl Tomola and Wolfgang Kurzer, escaped from Camp Scottsbluff and were not recaptured for over four months. They traveled all the way across the United States and Canada to the East Coast. They were finally captured by the FBI when they tried to ship out on a Spanish merchant ship from South Philadelphia, Pennsylvania. The escaped POWs were found hiding in empty oil drums on the ship's deck.[126]

CAMP SCOTTSBLUFF CLOSES

The first POWs started to leave Camp Scottsbluff in January 1946 to return to Europe. The last German prisoners left the camp on March 15, 1946. A small number of military staff and about twenty civilian employees remained at the camp to provide security for the camp property.[127]

After Camp Scottsbluff closed, several of the buildings were purchased and relocated by local businesses and farmers. The administrative building was moved to Minatare, Nebraska, in two separate parts and was used as the American Legion Hall, which was remodeled several years ago. Murals painted on several walls by POW Italian artist Rometi Pola were covered with siding. The building is currently privately owned and is operated as a restaurant and event hall. Remains of the former POW camp and structures include old concrete foundations. The site was used by the City of Scottsbluff as a landfill for many years and is currently used by the city for tree and yard waste.[128]

PART II

WYOMING BRANCH CAMPS AND POW LABOR

4

AGRICULTURAL BRANCH CAMPS
IN NORTH-CENTRAL WYOMING

BIG HORN COUNTY POW CAMPS

Three POW branch camps were established in Big Horn County to provide prisoner of war labor needed to assist area farmers in tending and harvesting their crops. Camp Basin and Camp Deaver both operated during 1944 and 1945. Both camps utilized former CCC camps that were renovated to house the prisoners of war. Camp Lovell operated only in 1945.[129]

CAMP BASIN, BIG HORN COUNTY

Camp Basin Operates in 1944–45

Camp Basin operated seasonally during 1944 and 1945. The number of prisoners at the camp fluctuated depending primarily on demands for sugar beet labor. The POW camp was located at the former CCC camp site. It is the current site of the Big Horn County Fairgrounds.[130]

A local newspaper article reported that prisoner of war labor would be handled through the Big Horn County Farm Labor Agency at the county agent's office in Basin. Farmers were advised to contact their local office to submit their request for labor needs. Beet growers paid the army directly for prisoner labor on the usual contract basis.[131]

Colonel H.K. Heath, commanding officer at Camp Douglas, visited the former CCC camp sites at Basin and Deaver in late April 1944. He approved both sites as being suitable for housing prisoners of war from Camp Douglas. The Big Horn County War Labor Agency requested 550 prisoners to provide labor for Big Horn County farmers. The prisoners were to be housed at the Basin and Deaver POW camps.[132]

In late September 1944, a group of 160 German prisoners were sent to Camp Basin from the Scottsbluff POW base camp. The prisoners assisted with the beet harvest.[133] The camp operated until the beet harvest was completed on November 7, 1944.[134]

On May 31, 1945, a local newspaper reported that 660 German prisoners would soon be working in Big Horn County. The prisoners were housed at the three POW camps in Basin, Deaver and Lovell. The necessity of thinning and harvesting every acre of beets planted was stressed due to the national sugar shortage.[135]

On June 1, 1945, the first prisoners returned to Camp Basin with several truckloads of supplies. Additional prisoners arrived the following day. There were 246 prisoners of war, with 18 guards at Camp Basin. Staff Sergeant Larry Willoughby was in charge of the Basin POW camp.[136]

By the end of July, the prisoners had completed thinning the beets. About 100 prisoners were sent to Camp Wheatland to work on area farms. There were 145 prisoners remaining at Camp Basin for hoeing beets and beans.[137]

A local newspaper announced that the beet harvest in Big Horn County would begin the end of September. The majority of the labor would be provided by the POWs housed at the three Big Horn County camps.[138] There were 245 German prisoners of war available to assist with the harvest. The sugar beet harvest was expected to be the largest ever grown in the area.[139] However, because of inclement weather, the beet crop did not meet expectations. The prisoners left Camp Basin after the beet harvest.[140] According to a local newspaper article, the Basin prisoner of war camp was considered outstanding for the quality and quantity of work conducted by the prisoners. The prisoners were "credited with a high record of accomplishment."[141]

Camp Basin POWs Describe the POW Camp and Surroundings

A former German POW described his home at the Basin POW camp as a "pleasant site": "Tall, shady poplars surround our seven barracks which,

Note the triangular formation of the barracks described by a Camp Basin POW at the former CCC/POW camp site. *Wyoming State Archives.*

in an orderly triangular arrangement, encompass a grassy place in the middle, on the tree lined edges of which many other cool, shady places can be found."[142]

The POW also described Basin as "a clean little town" "decorated with numerous parks and flower gardens." He remarked on the residences and "impressive buildings," such as the County Building, school and library. In addition, he mentioned the three bars in Basin—the POWs had to imagine what the interiors looked like.[143]

A poem written by another Basin POW, translated by Lowell Bangerter, described his perception of the Wyoming land near his camp at Basin:

> *In Wyoming Near Basin*
>
> *Immense, immeasurably great, this land,*
> *White peaks afar jut upward to the sky,*
> *Where clouds tear loose from them, from summits grand*
> *And their dark shadows wander o'er the throngs of high,*

Bleak, empty hills—of men completely free,—
As broad, as lonely as the distant sea.

Close to the river that flows through the plains
Presses itself a broad green strip of land
Which fields and meadows, houses and yard contains
Along the edge of fruitless barren sand.
It colors water that gives drink to fields,
Flies in the wind, when sun its hot breath yields.

The land is large and lies untamed and wild,
The thunder rumbles in the far ravine,
The lightning flashes in the darkness mild,
The storms rage through the deep bay, cold and mean.
Wild waters rush in fury downward bound
And drag so many to the grave's cold ground.

But when upon a happy sunny day
The tender breeze blows through the green trees there,
When man and beast in cooling shadows stay,
Then is the quiet land sunk down in prayer.
From distant peaks, untouched, caught in white glow,
One feels the breath of eternal snow.[144]

Basin Residents Share Their Memories

Several local residents shared their memories of the POW camp and prisoners. Barbara Greene recalled seeing the prisoners riding in the back of the big beet trucks when the farmers took them to the fields to work.[145] Tom Black remembered the prisoners being at the POW camp. He lived only about one half mile away. Black related that he would sometimes ride his small horse to the camp to see the prisoners. Some of the prisoners wanted to ride his horse. Black doesn't remember the prisoners being too heavily guarded, although there were guards walking around the camp. Black said that there were about one hundred men at the POW camp when he visited the prisoners.[146]

Local resident Bob Gish remembered interacting with the German prisoners at the Basin POW camp in the evenings after they were done

Former POW Camp Basin barracks, currently used as exhibit halls at the Big Horn County Fairgrounds. *Author's collection.*

working during 1944 and 1945. He was about fourteen years old, and he could talk with the prisoners through the fence that surrounded the camp. Gish said that it was very interesting speaking with them. He related that the prisoners did not want to go home. Gish described the prisoners as regular soldiers, "not SS." He reported that the prisoners were all ages, some as young as fifteen or sixteen. He recalled that most of them did not understand English, except a couple of the older men. Gish said the other prisoners learned to communicate over time. He remembered there were six or seven barracks buildings at the former POW camp site and that the guards lived in one of the buildings.[147]

In May 1946, a local newspaper reported that the former POW/CCC camp became Basin's property. The entire camp property was transferred from the Bureau of Reclamation to Basin without charge. The bureau's application for the camp buildings was withdrawn, acknowledging the "dire need for local housing units" in Basin.[148] Three former POW camp barracks are still used at the Big Horn County Fairgrounds as exhibit halls.[149]

CAMP LOVELL, BIG HORN COUNTY

Camp Lovell Operates in 1945

Camp Lovell operated from May 1945 through early November 1945. The first prisoners sent to Camp Lovell worked on remodeling the armory building and cavalry barn to house the prisoners of war. The Lovell Armory was constructed in 1923 of steel and sheet iron and was approximately 60 feet wide and 140 feet long. Partial concrete flooring was one of the modifications undertaken to update the former cavalry barn for prisoner use.[150] The prisoners were sent from Camp Deaver until the remodeling was completed. In late May, the *Lovell Chronicle* reported that work on the armory building and cavalry barn at Lovell to house approximately two hundred prisoners was progressing rapidly.[151]

POWs Work in Lovell Area

In early June 1945, approximately two hundred German prisoners arrived at Camp Lovell from Camp Douglas, primarily to assist with thinning the local beet crop. Prisoner labor was made available by the War Food Administration and the Big Horn County Labor Agency. The prisoners of war were shipped through the cooperation of the Wyoming Extension Service and the U.S. Army POW camp at Douglas.[152]

The prisoners completed thinning the sugar beets in late July. Some POWs assisted with other agricultural work.[153] The prisoners returned to the camp to help with the beet harvest in late September. They left Camp Lovell and returned to Camp Scottsbluff in early November 1945.[154]

Lovell-Area Residents Remember the POW Camp and Prisoners

Thales Haskell delivered two hundred to three hundred loaves of bread from Brown's Bakery to the Lovell POW camp each day. He remembered three or four guard towers and a fence around the area for the POWs to exercise in.[155] Another area resident, Peggy Luthy, recalled the prisoners digging a ditch for plumbing into the beauty shop in Lovell. She said the POWs were always polite.[156] Lovell resident Rich Fink remembered his mother telling him that some German prisoners crawled under the fence at night and went to a local bar.[157]

Lovell Armory with cavalry troops prior to being modified for use for the Camp Lovell prisoners of war. *Wyoming National Guard Museum.*

The prisoners worked on the Tippetts' farm in Lovell. According to Thomas Tippetts, the POWs were hired by his father, Marion Tippetts, to help with the beet harvest. The prisoners also dug a well and constructed a shop and corrals. In addition, they unloaded and spread gypsum on the fields to neutralize the alkaline salt, which made the fields more productive. The Tippetts family kept in touch with one of the former prisoners, Paul Stauga, after the war. One family member visited Stauga in Germany.[158]

Gary Goodrich shared his childhood memories of the German prisoners. Goodrich lived and worked on his aunt and uncle's (Della and Leroy Tippetts) farm southwest of Lovell. His uncle employed ten to fifteen prisoners, accompanied by a guard, to work in the sugar beet fields. Goodrich said the prisoners traded cigarettes and pens with the guards. Even though his aunt had lost her son because of the war, she treated the prisoners with compassion. After the prisoners completed their work for the day, his aunt served the prisoners strawberries mixed with "precious rationed" sugar and cream for dessert. Goodrich recalled the prisoners and guard smiling at the "unexpected kindness." When the prisoners finished eating, they would line up, bow and say "danke." Goodrich remembered that one prisoner stood to the side and did not thank his aunt.[159]

Local resident Tim Townsend recalled the prisoners working on his parents' farm east of Lovell. Townsend was about ten years old. His parents raised pinto beans. His father would pick up and drop off about eight prisoners when he needed help with the beans. The POWs stacked the beans in piles to dry and loaded the beans into the wagon for threshing.

Camp Lovell POWs on farm equipment at the Tippetts' farm. *Courtesy Judy Wray and Thomas Tippetts.*

Townsend said that some of the prisoners could speak broken English and that they were "congenial and friendly." Townsend related a story about watching the prisoners working one day when they found a good-sized rattlesnake. They killed the snake, made a fire, roasted the snake and ate it! The prisoners offered him some, but Townsend said he was not interested in eating the snake.[160]

Former Camp Lovell POW Returns to Live in Area

After the war, one former prisoner from Camp Lovell, Robert Schultz, and his wife and sons moved to Lovell to live. He later moved to Cowley and lived there for many years. Schultz had been sent to Camp Lovell as a war prisoner in the spring of 1945 and worked primarily in the area beet fields. He was sponsored by Mr. and Mrs. Willie Korrel, Kamiel Wambeke and George Wambeke of Lovell. Schultz worked for Willie Korrel when he returned to Wyoming. He also worked in construction for several years and for Great Western Sugar.[161]

CAMP DEAVER, BIG HORN COUNTY

Camp Deaver Operates at Former CCC Camp

Camp Deaver operated seasonally from June 1944 through October 1945. The prisoners worked on area farms in the Deaver, Frannie and Cowley areas. The majority of work was with sugar beets, although the prisoners also weeded beans, put up hay and did other farmwork.[162]

The prisoners were housed in the former CCC camp, which had been renovated for the POWs in early 1944. The camp was approved to house up to three hundred prisoners.[163] There were eight barracks and a few smaller buildings.[164] A floodlight system and barbed-wire fence enclosure around the camp were installed.[165] The wooden barracks were painted green. There were about ten to twelve guards assigned to the camp, and they lived in one separate building.[166]

In June 1944, 110 German POWs were sent to Camp Deaver from Camp Scottsbluff to work in the local beet fields.[167] They returned to Camp Deaver in the fall to harvest the beet crop. During the harvest, area landowner

The Deaver POW camp operated at this former CCC camp site and utilized the barracks for housing the POWs. *Regional National Archives, Broomfield, Colorado, courtesy Robert Audretsch.*

Carl Hessenthaler realized that one of the POWs working in his fields was his nephew, whose family lived in Germany. Camp Deaver closed in early November 1944 after the beet harvest was completed.[168]

From early June through mid-July 1945, approximately 235 prisoners were sent to Camp Deaver from the Camp Douglas base camp to work in the beet fields. The prisoners returned to Camp Deaver in late September to harvest the beets.[169] The prisoners completed their work and left Camp Deaver on October 31, 1945.[170]

The Camp Deaver prisoners requested musical instruments and a piano to use during their free time. The POWs formed a band. Residents who lived nearby enjoyed listening to the prisoners play and sing in the evenings after they returned to the camp.[171]

Area Resident Writes Book About Camp Deaver

Area resident Johanna Gimmeson wrote a book, *German POW Camp in Deaver, Wyoming, 1944–1945*, that contains details about the POW camp and interviews with local residents about the prisoners and the work they did. Gimmeson recalled the prisoners working on her parents' farm in the beet fields and helping to remodel their house. She particularly remembered Joseph, a carpenter, who spoke English. Joseph was captured in Poland but forced to join the German army. After the war, her family kept in touch with him and sent him food packages to help him during the postwar shortages and hard times in his country.[172]

Local Residents Provide Memories and Details About the POW Camp and Prisoners

Several area residents shared their memories of the POWs working on local farms. Longtime Deaver resident Fred Wambeke said that the POW camp barracks buildings extended down their road on the east side of Deaver. Their current property includes the former cook tent area. Wambeke remembered his father picking up the German POWs in his truck and taking them to the sugar beet fields. Wambeke recalled that his mother felt sorry for the prisoners and made them marmalade sandwiches and would visit with them.[173]

Deaver POW Ernst Ruehling painted a landscape as a gift to a Frannie, Wyoming resident. *Homesteader Museum Collection.*

Cowley resident Paul Lewis related that his father would drive six miles to Deaver to pick up prisoners to work on his farm. Lewis remembered fifteen to twenty prisoners with one guard. The guard sat up front with Lewis and his father; the prisoners sat in the back. They brought two big insulated pans with sandwiches for lunch. Lewis's father provided the POWs with water and had to pay for the prisoners to work. The prisoners had large *PW* letters printed on their clothes. Lewis recalled that his father had a pocket watch that he had to wind several times a day. One of the prisoners, a jeweler, noticed the problems he was having with his watch. The prisoner made a new mainspring. Lewis's father had to wind his watch just once a day after that. Lewis said that they had no problems with the prisoners.[174]

Stanley Partridge remembered the German prisoners working on his father's farm. Partridge went with his father to pick up prisoners to work sugar beets on a farm his father rented north of Cowley. Partridge was eleven or twelve years old when the Deaver camp operated. He related that sugar beets were very labor intensive then, and the prisoners would hoe weeds and thin the beets. The prisoners brought their lunches with them. He recalled one very hot day when the prisoners asked the guard if they could swim in a pond on the farm. The guard said "yes" and handed Partridge his carbine with his ammunition and went swimming, too. Partridge said that the guards treated the prisoners well. The guard would speak to the prisoners, and the prisoners knew enough English to get by. Partridge said there was no animosity between them.[175]

Longtime Frannie resident Buck Homewood said that between eight and twelve prisoners worked on his family's farm. Homewood recalled a German prisoner telling him that he was given the choice to "join the German army or get shot!" His dad brought the prisoners up to the house for lunch. The prisoners ate outside; his mother brought out extra food such as cookies and coffee. His mother was good to the POWs. A prisoner painted an oil picture of a landscape with mountains in the background for her. The painting is on display at the Homesteader Museum in Powell.[176] The artist was Ernst Ruehling, who was twenty-one years old when he painted the picture.[177]

Len Brightly recalled riding by the Deaver POW camp a number of times. He remembered eight to nine barracks in rows pointing north and south. Brightly said the POW camp compound was enclosed by a high fence with strands of barbed wire. He remembered seeing about eight to ten "Nazi soldiers" on the west side of the camp. The prisoners were marching in formation and "goose stepping" along the fence line. The soldiers would "click their heels together sharply each time they stopped," which was "kind of scary" to a young boy.[178]

The Brightly family lived on a farm between Deaver and Cowley, where his father raised sugar beets. His father picked up about twelve prisoners and one guard from the Deaver POW camp to help on the farm. Brightly remembered the guard slept in the ditch with his rifle while the prisoners worked.[179] Another area resident, Dennis Godfrey, remembered the guards who came to their farm sitting under the trees reading or "exercising their guns on rabbits and prairie dogs."[180]

Brightly said his family got to know the prisoners very well. His father spoke some German and was very happy with the work the prisoners did. Brightly and his two older brothers liked to watch the prisoners working in the fields. At noon, the boys would join their father and the prisoners for lunch. Brightly's mother would fix the boys sack lunches with homemade bread and peanut butter and jelly with canned fruit. The prisoners had "store bought bread" with cheese and bologna. Brightly said the boys seldom had bread or sliced meat from the store. The prisoners and boys envied what each other brought for lunch, so they traded lunches. One day, Brightly's mother made spaghetti patties and fried them for the boys. Brightly said that when the prisoners saw the spaghetti patties, they all wanted them and "they almost fought over who got to trade with us."[181]

A former Camp Deaver barracks still stands at the former POW camp site. *Author's collection.*

Brightly remembered that one evening around midnight the boys heard a knock at the door and voices. Then the lights came on, so they got up. His mom had a pot of coffee on the stove and was baking a cake. Their late-night guests were some German prisoners from Camp Deaver. They had climbed over the fence and walked from the camp to the farm. The war was over, and they were going to be shipped to another location the next day, so they came to say goodbye to his mother and father. The POWs stayed as long as they could but said they needed to get back over the fence before it got light. The prisoners left and walked back to the POW camp.[182]

Brightly described a small wooden box made by one of the prisoners, Karl Biltman, for his father. The prisoner used the end of a wood fruit box and carved a picture of the Big Horn Mountains with a mountain sheep on it and the sun rising in the background. Brightly was told the POW used a sharpened bedspring to carve the wood.[183]

After the war, some of the barracks buildings were moved to other locations in the Deaver area. Renovated buildings were previously used for a town hall and library and by the Deaver Rod and Gun Club for a clubhouse. A former barracks building still exits on the POW camp site and is used for storage today.[184]

CAMP POWELL, PARK COUNTY

A Small, Short-Term Camp Operates in Powell

Camp Powell (Powell Branch Camp No. 9) operated only from October 12, 1945, to November 5, 1945. A small group of forty-four German POWs were sent from Camp Douglas to work during the beet harvest. The prisoners were housed in the American Legion Community Log Building (now the Homesteader Museum) until they were relocated to the Deaver POW camp.[185]

According to a local newspaper report, on October 18, 1945, about forty German POWs were being housed in the barracks on the grounds of the Legion Hall. The guards were housed in the Boy Scout cabin located adjacent to the enclosure. Local farmers reported that the prisoners were proving to be a great help in the beet labor needs.[186]

Local resident Willie Eggerbrecht served as a guard for the German POWs at the former American Legion building. He escorted the prisoners

Camp Powell American Legion Community Log Building that housed POWs during the short-term operation of the camp. *Homesteader Museum Collection.*

to and from the camp each day to the area fields to work. Eggerbrecht had also worked with the German prisoners at the Rogers bean mill, sorting beans.[187]

German prisoners had previously been sent to Powell to work from Camp Deaver in 1944. A local newspaper article specified that forty-seven German prisoners were working at the bean mills in Powell and a few POWs were assisting farmers with crop harvests. Managers at the local bean mills reported that, although most of the German prisoners were from cities and had little farmwork experience, they were good workers.[188]

The Camp Powell guard quarters had previously served as a church. The cabin was located east of the Homesteader Museum, where the Powell Chamber of Commerce is currently located. The building was moved to a new location in Powell and is now a private residence.[189]

CAMP WORLAND, WASHAKIE COUNTY

Italian Prisoners Arrive at Camp Worland during Fall 1943

The first group of two hundred Italian prisoners of war arrived at the Worland POW camp by train on September 30, 1943. The prisoners were housed at the former CCC camp. They were sent to Camp Worland from Camp Douglas to assist with the local harvest of the sugar beet crop.[190]

Modifications and updates to the former CCC camp necessary for its use as a prisoner of war camp were made. A woven wire fence was installed around the camp. The buildings were cleaned, the plumbing was repaired and the weeds were cut.[191] The U.S. Army personnel and prisoners were housed in separate barracks. In addition, there were separate mess halls for the enlisted men and the prisoners. The camp commander identified specific buildings at the POW camp on camp photos he took, including the noncommissioned officers' quarters, an orderly room, the enlisted men's barracks and a sentry shelter.[192]

According to a local newspaper, the prisoners "fell into ranks" at the Worland depot "and marched four abreast to their new quarters." They wore blue denim work clothes that had large yellow letters *WP* painted on their jacket sleeves and pant legs. The Italian soldiers were heard talking and laughing in their native language soon after they arrived.[193]

On October 1, 1943, the Camp Worland war prisoners started work. Approximately 150 POWs worked in the local beet fields to help top beets. Other prisoners worked at the camp. The prisoners were reported to be in good spirits and seemed eager to work.[194]

The beet harvest was completed in the first week of November 1943. The Italian POWs and the American military staff returned to Camp Douglas. Holly Sugar Corporation officials reported that the Italian prisoners of war "helped a great deal in getting the sugar beet crops harvested," in spite of being inexperienced and working only eight hours a day.[195]

German Prisoners Arrive in 1944

On June 9, 1944, the first group of one hundred German prisoners of war arrived at Camp Worland to work in the area beet fields. They had been sent from Camp Scottsbluff. The prisoners were provided through the cooperation of the U.S. War Department and the Washakie County Beet Growers Association.[196]

However, less than two weeks later, ninety-four of the German prisoners went on strike and refused to work in the Worland area fields. The strike was attributed to the POWs' reaction to a change from daywork to piecework pay rates. The prisoners protested specific living and working conditions at Camp Worland. They complained about not having benches in the trucks that transported them to and from their work sites, a leaking roof in one of the buildings and the lack of a sports field. Six other prisoners working at the camp also supported their comrades in the strike. Administrative action was taken by army officials. The prisoners were placed on a reduced diet of bread and water in accordance with Geneva Convention guidelines for punishment for the disobedience of direct orders pertaining to prisoner labor.[197]

The strike at Camp Worland made national headlines.[198] A local newspaper reported that the striking prisoners appealed to Adolf Hitler in a written communication they composed for help in meeting their demands. However, the Camp Scottsbluff commander reported that there was no evidence that a written appeal was made.[199] After five days on bread and water, the strike ended. The German prisoners agreed to return to their work in the beet fields, and they were provided with full food rations.[200]

The prisoners completed their summer work in the beet fields in mid-July 1944. They returned to the Scottsbluff POW base camp the following day.[201] During the fall of 1944, two hundred prisoners were sent back to Camp Worland to help with the local beet harvest.[202]

German Prisoners Provide the Majority of Labor for Beet Harvest

Approximately three hundred German prisoners of war were sent from Camp Douglas to Camp Worland to assist with the sugar beet crop in 1945.[203] German prisoners first returned to Camp Worland in May to work in the beet fields.[204] The prisoners were sent back to the POW camp again in the first week of October 1945 to assist during the beet harvest.[205] A severe storm ended the Worland area beet harvest in early November with only about 75 percent of normal sugar beet yields.[206] The prisoners of war were credited with providing more than 57 percent of the labor in the 1945 harvest of Washakie County's sugar beets, valued at $673,545.[207]

Local Residents Provide Details About Camp Worland

Local resident Gerry Geis provided details about the POW camp located at the former CCC camp. He recalled the wood barracks and the fence that was installed around the POW camp.[208] Another area resident, Lloyd

German POWs working in the sugar beet fields near Worland. *Washakie Museum and Cultural Center.*

Lungren, related information about the location of the POW camp and the prisoners. He said that both the Italian and German prisoners worked on area farms.[209]

After the war, several of the former barracks used at the POW camp were moved across the tracks to lower Howell Avenue. The buildings were converted into apartments to provide readily available housing during the severe housing shortage that developed in the Worland area after the war.[210] According to longtime Worland resident Clint Corneal, his father moved the former barracks to Sixth Street and Howell, where they are currently used as apartments. In addition, some other former POW camp buildings were moved outside of Worland for use by area farmers and still stand today.[211]

Former Prisoner of War Returns to Visit Worland

Former German POW Wolfran Suetter returned to Worland with his son to visit the Adam and Lloyd Lungren families in 1983. Suetter was a prisoner sent to Camp Worland from Camp Douglas in May 1945 to help with the sugar beet crop. Suetter described the work the prisoners did in the area fields. He said the POWs thinned the beets using short-handled hoes. He remembered that it was hard work, but after they got used to it, "it wasn't too bad."[212]

Suetter said that he returned to Germany with lifetime memories of Wyoming, including the size of the fields, the irrigation methods and the use of three-wheeled tractors. He passed his memories on to his children, who all spent time in the United States.[213] Worland native Lloyd Lungren related that Wolfran Suetter worked on his father's farm. After the war, Lungren's family visited Suetter and his family in Germany.[214]

CLEARMONT POW CAMP, SHERIDAN COUNTY

Camp Clearmont Operates in 1945

The Clearmont POW camp was established in 1945, primarily to help local farmers with the sugar beet crop. However, the prisoners did other work in the Clearmont area, including haying and house painting. The camp was activated on June 4, 1945. Approximately 250 German prisoners of war were sent to Camp Clearmont from Camp Scottsbluff to work thinning beets and in the hay fields on local farms. The camp was temporarily inactivated on August 4, 1945, after the work was completed. On August 14, the camp was reactivated; 200 prisoners returned to Camp Clearmont from Camp Douglas to help harvest the sugar beet crop. The Clearmont POW camp closed on November 3, 1945, after the harvest was completed.[215]

Local farmers organized the Sheridan County Farm Labor Agency to obtain labor for sugar beet production in the county. The prisoners were housed in the former CCC camp barracks that had been moved to Clearmont from Gillette. The camp was located on land leased from the Holly Sugar Company adjacent to Clear Creek on the Art Roebling ranch. The buildings were set on foundations, and a sewer and water system was installed. A ten-foot-high fence was constructed around the camp.[216]

Clearmont-Area Residents Share Their Memories

Local farmers drove to the POW camp in the mornings to pick up their quota of prisoners and took them to the fields to work. A U.S. Army guard was assigned to each group of prisoners. After work, the farmers returned the prisoners to the camp by 5:00 p.m. The prisoners' lunches, prepared at the camp, "consisted of a piece of bread, a slice of lunch meat and an apple." Many farmers also provided hot lunches and snacks for the prisoners.[217]

According to area farmers, the prisoners worked hard to keep up their morale. They sang when they returned to the camp in the evenings. Camp-area neighbors enjoyed listening to the voices of the German prisoners singing in harmony.[218]

Clearmont residents reported that the prisoners were hard workers and very polite, and that most of them were well educated. Security was not strict at the camp. One POW was sent to the post office alone on a regular basis. One German sergeant even served as the unofficial football coach at the school. Local residents watched the prisoners play soccer in the evenings and on Sundays. They related that many of the farmers made friends with the prisoners and communicated with them after they returned to Germany.[219]

Zach Garretson worked with his grandparents on the Claud and Cora Bolinger Ranch in Ucross as a young boy. The Bolingers raised sugar beets. Garretson was responsible for herding the milk cows to graze the grass along the railroad tracks. He remembered the German prisoners working in the field next to where he watched the cows. Armed guards in the corners of the field watched over the ten to twelve prisoners. Garretson related that Claud Bolinger told him that former prisoners from Camp Clearmont came back to visit him after the war.[220]

According to Claud Bolinger, during the fall sugar beet harvest, they needed to work seven days a week due to a family member injury and the threat of early snow. However, the prisoners were not required to work on Sundays. So, Cora Bolinger offered to serve the prisoners a big Sunday dinner if they would work. The prisoners agreed, and the beet harvest was completed on time.[221]

The POW camp at Clearmont had a good doctor whom some of the local residents went to. A local young man developed a serious foot fungus condition. He was treated at the infirmary at the University of Wyoming, where he attended college. He also went to Denver for treatment, but the soreness on the bottom of his foot was not resolved. He had trouble walking and spent most of his time lying down. The prisoners felt sorry for him and advised him to see the POW camp doctor. The doctor treated him with medicine to soak his feet in several times a day, and within a few weeks, he was cured.[222]

The Fowlers Share POW Photo and Letters

Rose and John Fowler employed about fourteen prisoners to work on their farm in the sugar beet fields. Rose set up tables on the lawn and fed them a hot noon meal and "plenty of bread, peanut butter and honey" to supplement the sack lunch prepared for them at the camp. She remembered that the prisoners especially enjoyed the peanut butter. When the weather turned cold, the prisoners ate inside the house in the dining room.[223]

Rose Fowler took a photo of the prisoners on the last day they worked on their ranch. The prisoners smiled for the picture, and she offered to send all the POWs a copy of the photo after they returned to their homes. Some of the POWs wrote to the Fowlers after the war and provided details about the war-torn country and damaged homes they returned to. The prisoners also related how many POWs were sent to England to work, sometimes for up to two years after leaving the U.S. POW camps, before finally being returned to Germany.[224]

Rose shared some of letters they received after the war from the former prisoners who had worked on the ranch. One of the prisoners who wrote her told how he was "shocked by the sight of the conditions" in Germany.

Clearmont POWs on the last day they worked on the Fowler farm. *Photo by Rose Fowler. Sheridan County Museum.*

He said their house was badly "destroyed by explosives and fire bombs." The roof leaked water into the rooms, but the damages could not be repaired, because there were no materials available. The worst problem they faced was the "horrible food situation." He said the famine was hard to image. His mother weighed 88 pounds, and his father's weight dropped from 178 to 114 pounds. The former prisoner hadn't been able to find a job. He said that even though it wasn't "an easy life behind barbed wire, he was still better off in the U.S. as far as food and clothing."[225]

Clearmont POW Camp After the War

After the war, the camp was deactivated and the buildings were torn down or sold and moved. Some of the former buildings still survive in the Clearmont area. One local resident bought a barracks building and used it to erect a home in Clearmont that still stands today.[226] Two of the former barracks buildings were used to construct the main section of the Red Arrow Café, which was torn down in 2017. One of the buildings was relocated onto a local resident's property.[227] There are no remains of the camp structures at the former POW camp site. The site was restored to its former condition and is currently used as pasture.[228]

5

AGRICULTURAL AND TIMBER BRANCH CAMPS IN WEST-CENTRAL WYOMING

CAMP RIVERTON, FREMONT COUNTY

Camp Riverton Operates in 1945

Camp Riverton operated from June into early November 1945. In early June, a group of 104 German prisoners of war arrived at the Riverton POW camp. The POWs were sent from the Camp Douglas base camp. They returned to Camp Douglas on November 5, 1945, after the beet harvest was completed.[229] The Riverton POW camp was located at the former armory, south of West Adams Road, with the entrance on the west side.[230]

The Riverton Armory, a wood-frame building constructed in 1925, included stables. The armory site was inspected by army officers from Camp Scottsbluff in early March 1945 to determine what modifications were needed for the prisoner of war camp. Approximately one hundred prisoners were approved for assignment to Camp Riverton.[231]

The prisoners were housed in the armory building, which was remodeled by a local contractor. Renovations included the construction of a partition in the armory building, a guard house, an infirmary, latrines and additional plumbing. Remodeling costs, estimated at $2,200, were shared by the State Extension Service and the Holly Sugar Corporation. Local farmers were responsible for constructing a fence around the facility.[232] Riverton resident Tony Swasso described the former armory

Riverton Armory building, which housed the Camp Riverton prisoners of war in 1945. *Wyoming National Guard Museum.*

building as a large, two-story, white, wood, rectangular building with a domed roof. When the POW camp operated at the site, the camp was surrounded by a high fence.[233]

Camp Riverton POWs Work on Area Farms

The prisoners primarily thinned beets, did general farmwork and harvested the bean and beet crops. Farmers picked up the prisoners from the camp in the morning and returned them at night. A guard was assigned to each group of prisoners that left the camp.[234] The prisoners also assisted in local area construction projects, which included building a house in Paradise Valley.[235]

There were about 1,800 acres of beets in the Riverton area to be harvested in the fall of 1945. After the beet harvest, the beets were trucked to the Holly Sugar Corporation beet factory in Worland. A group of POWs was scheduled to leave the Riverton camp to work elsewhere, but the joint efforts of the Holly Sugar Corporation and the Riverton Chamber of Commerce kept the prisoners at the Riverton POW camp to do other area farmwork until the beet harvest was completed.[236] Additional prisoners were requested to work in the Riverton area, but there was a shortage of POWs to meet labor needs.[237]

Bob and Paul Sauer, longtime Riverton residents, recalled prisoners working in the fields on the farm their parents operated west of Riverton. Bob Sauer was thirteen years old when the Riverton POW camp was in operation. He remembered that the prisoners used to love to talk with his mother in German about where they were from.[238] Paul Sauer remembered riding his horse to see the prisoners working in the sugar beet fields. He recalled about six to seven prisoners working on the farm accompanied by one guard. Their mother used to fry chicken for the prisoners, who ate inside the house.[239]

Fritz Rein remembered working with the German prisoners of war on the Bill Mund farm in Riverton. Mund picked up three prisoners from the POW camp at the armory to work on his farm. Rein and his brother had a contract with Mund for threshing grain, and the prisoners worked with them to feed the threshing machine. The farmers were not supposed to feed the prisoners, but they did because the prisoners worked hard. Mund sent plates out to the prisoners at lunchtime. They ate in the milk barn. Rein speaks German, so he could communicate with them. He related that a prisoner said they either had to serve in the German army or get shot.[240]

Local resident Gayle Currah recalled that his father also used prisoners of war to help on his farm in Missouri Valley. Currah said the prisoners helped with the irrigation and the bean and grain harvests. He remembered that his family treated the prisoners well. The prisoners ate at his family's table and "did not have to eat just the sack lunches they were provided with."[241]

CAMP DUBOIS, FREMONT COUNTY

Camp Dubois Operates at Isolated Location

Camp Dubois was established at the request of the Wyoming Tie and Timber Company.[242] The POW timber camp operated seasonally from July 1944 into mid-January 1946 (a total of about fourteen months). Camp Dubois was located at a very isolated site within the forest near the timber that needed to be cut, primarily to make railroad ties. Up to 150 German prisoners, sent from the Camp Scottsbluff base camp, worked at the POW

Overview of Camp Dubois POW timber camp surrounded by the forest. *Photo by Lieutenant Harold Harlamert, courtesy Electric Consumer.*

camp, along with U.S. military personnel. The number of POWs assigned to the camp fluctuated during the year, depending on the labor needed for specific jobs.[243]

The Camp Dubois POW camp was located southwest of Dubois, near the headwaters of Little Warm Spring Creek, within the Shoshone National Forest. The camp was located at an elevation of about nine thousand feet, so weather conditions at the camp throughout the year were often severe. Winter temperatures sometimes dropped to twenty degrees below zero. Camp Dubois was completely snowed in, and access was cut off several times during the camp operation in the fall and winter months. Sometimes, the only way to reach the camp with supplies was by horse and sled from the Wyoming Tie and Timber Company headquarters eight miles away.[244]

Camp Dubois U.S. Military Personnel

Lieutenant Harold Harlamert was the camp commander from October 1944 to January 15, 1946, when Camp Dubois closed. According to Harlamert, in December 1944, there were 10 enlisted U.S. military personnel assigned to the site and a maximum of 150 prisoners. In 1945, the number of enlisted men assigned to the site dropped to 7, with 138 prisoners. He reported that the prisoners were very cooperative and never caused trouble.[245] Harlamert felt "it was a privilege" to have the camp commander assignment at the Dubois camp. He loved the primitiveness and isolation of the camp. However, he had serious concerns about being snowed in and feeding the men he was responsible for on limited supplies. Therefore, during the fall and winter months, Harlamert ordered an extra week's supply of rations.[246]

Harlamert provided detailed military reports and records, including information about the number of U.S. military personnel and prisoners assigned to the site, the POW camp site, details of the residents' accommodations and the work conducted by the POWs. In addition, the camp commander set up a weather station at the camp and monitored weather conditions daily. Harlamert's extensive record keeping, correspondence and photos contribute greatly to understanding the details of how Camp Dubois operated.[247]

Camp activities and recreation for both the U.S. military staff and the prisoners were limited at the isolated timber camp. The lights were turned off at 10:00 p.m. every evening, so both American personnel and POWs usually spent quiet evenings reading, writing, playing cards or playing their musical instruments. The camp commander wrote about his excitement when Ricker Van Metre, president of the Wyoming Tie and Timber Company, lent him a radio to help pass the long evenings. Unfortunately, a defective switch caused a short in the camp's limited lighting system, which burned out bulbs, melted light sockets and set the radio on fire.[248] Harlamert and some of the enlisted men enjoyed several outdoor activities, including hunting and fishing during their time off.[249]

The Camp Dubois enlisted men served as clerks, guards and drivers. Camp records show that the camp was not heavily guarded, based primarily on its isolated location. U.S. enlisted men James Swift and Harold Olson were the unofficial camp fishermen. Harlamert noted that they seldom left camp on leave, other than an occasional trip to get supplies. They were dedicated fishermen and spent all their spare time fishing. The camp commander went fishing with them when he could. When he couldn't get away, he sent the enlisted men to fish to supplement their rations. Harlamert reported that they usually ate fish three times a week.[250]

The U.S. military staff created their own fun when they could. This included one of the camp guards, Eno Fraterelli. Harlamert relates a story about the enlisted men dressing up like cowboys. There had been a cattle drive through the area, and the men asked the cowboys if they could dress up in their chaps and cowboy hats and use their gear and horses for camp

Camp Dubois guard posing as a cowboy for camp photos. *Photo by Lieutenant Harold Harlamert, courtesy Linda Siemens.*

photos. Fraterelli even asked the camp commander to borrow his revolver and holster to make the photos look more realistic.[251]

One Camp Dubois enlisted man, Luther Morris, was killed in a truck rollover accident on December 21, 1944. The accident occurred about twenty miles east of Dubois on a supply run to Riverton. Two other enlisted men riding in the truck were injured but survived.[252]

Camp Dubois Timber Work

According to Harlamert, Camp Dubois prisoners worked cutting down trees in the forest with two-man crosscut saws. They dragged logs from the logging sites to the area sawmills with teams of horses. The POWs worked at the sawmills, cutting, stacking and loading the railroad ties onto trucks, which transported them down to the Wind River, where they were stacked. In the spring, the ties were bulldozed into the river, where they would be floated down to Riverton (about eighty-five miles) to the creosoting plant on the annual "tie drive."[253]

Camp Dubois POWs worked with civilian loggers in the forest and at the sawmills. One concern Harlamert shared was his frustration with the civilian workers who supplied the POWs with liquor. Harlamert relates an incident that occurred in November 1945:

> *Saturday afternoon I had a little change of routine in camp life. One of the PWs came in at noon—dead drunk. Upon checking, I discovered that the other 3 PWs that worked at the same mill, had come into camp, removed their outer coats* [which identified them as PWs], *leaving them in camp and were gone. Further checking revealed that the saw mill was not operating. Upon questioning the civilian saw mill operator's wife, she stated that he had gone down to a beer joint about 10 miles west of Dubois. One of the truck drivers had seen the PWs riding down the hill with the civilian. Putting two and two together, I surmised that the civilian had taken the PWs to the tavern with him.*
>
> *Not wishing to be embarrassed by three of my PWs being found, possibly drunk, in a public tavern, you can imagine my haste in taking off after them. We were almost at the foot of the hill, when, sure enough, here comes the civilian with the PWs in his car. He tried to explain that he had meant no harm, but because of the good work the boys did for him he wanted to show his appreciation and buy them a little beer. I acted as if I was pretty mad and told him I would see him Monday morning.*[254]

The camp commander reprimanded the civilian supervisor. He visited the sawmills and advised the operators that any further passing out of liquor to the prisoners would result in instant and permanent withdrawal of all PWs from the mills. He warned the prisoners that if they got caught accepting liquor from civilian workers, they would be subject to two weeks of bread and water.[255]

However, it was not the first time Camp Dubois POWs left the camp to have a few beers with civilian workers. One former Camp Dubois prisoner reported visiting a local roadhouse. He recalled how the prisoners enjoyed occasional excursions to the bar with the civilian loggers.[256]

The only other time the camp commander's records indicated the POWs were warned of the severe punishment of a restricted diet of bread and water was if the prisoners were ever caught smoking in the woods. Due to the camp's isolated location within the forest, Harlamert was very concerned with the potential for fire to spread quickly throughout the camp. Therefore, the prisoners were warned not to smoke while working in the woods because of the extreme fire danger.[257]

The POW Camp

The design and construction of Camp Dubois utilized the existing site conditions, natural resources and topography at the site. Site plans and photographs of the Camp Dubois POW camp and individual buildings provide detailed information about the camp. In addition, military reports, interviews and correspondence provide additional information about how the camp operated.[258]

There were separate wood-framed mess halls, washrooms and latrines for the American military personnel and POWs. A small stream that ran through the camp provided drinking and washing water. The camp had electric lights powered by two light plants. The POW tents, wash buildings and latrines were secured in the enclosed fenced area during the war.[259] However, according to a former prisoner account, the POWs were not fenced in during the last summer and fall that the camp operated.[260]

The "Main Street" ran through the center of the camp from the entrance road and led to the enlisted men's area. It also divided the camp. East of the Main Street was the enclosed POW living area, consisting of their tents, latrines and wash area. There were thirty-six sixteen-foot-by-sixteen-foot tents for the prisoners, including an infirmary tent. In addition, there were

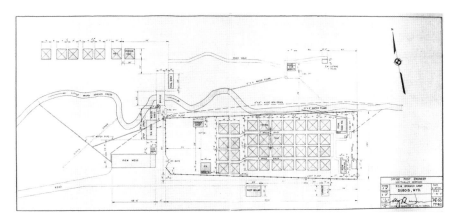

The Camp Dubois site plan depicts the location and details of the camp buildings, tents and roads. *U.S. War Department, June 1945, courtesy Linda Siemens.*

smaller tents designated as the PX and barber tents. On the west side of the Main Street, other camp buildings were located, such as the mess halls.[261] The use of both the infirmary and barber tents was documented in Camp Dubois records and interviews.[262]

Harlamert described the POW camp accommodations in great detail. The prisoners, enlisted men and the camp commander were housed in wood-framed tents covered with large canvas. There were four POWS assigned to each tent. There were usually two enlisted men assigned to a tent. The camp commander had his own private tent. A wood-burning stove was located in the center of each tent. There were seven tents within the U.S. military staff portion of the camp, which included the headquarters tent and a storage tent.[263]

The POW kitchen and mess hall was the largest structure at the camp. The wood building was about twenty-one feet wide by sixty-nine feet long. Water was piped into both the POW and enlisted men kitchens from a nearby creek and discharged into a box drain below the camp. Both kitchens had ice refrigerators.[264] In 1945, an electric refrigerator was installed adjacent to the POW kitchen and mess hall to help reduce meat spoilage.[265] During the final breakdown of Camp Dubois in January 1946, the POW kitchen and mess hall housed the thirty-two POWs still left working at the camp.[266]

The enlisted men's kitchen and mess hall was a smaller wood building that measured about sixteen feet by thirty feet.[267] According to Harlamert, during the final breakdown of the camp, both the enlisted men and the POWs shared

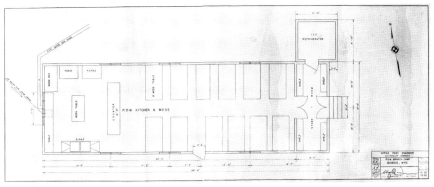

This page, top: Camp Dubois POWs and guard outside the POW mess hall. *Photo by Lieutenant Harold Harlamert, courtesy Linda Siemens.*

This page, bottom: POW kitchen and mess hall site plans show details of the building. *U.S. War Department, June 1945, courtesy Linda Siemens.*

Opposite, top: Camp Dubois "Main Street." *Photo by Lieutenant Harold Harlamert, courtesy Linda Siemens.*

Opposite, middle: Camp Dubois tents at the isolated timber camp. *Photo by Lieutenant Harold Harlamert, courtesy Linda Siemens.*

Opposite, bottom: A view inside the Camp Dubois commander's tent. *Photo by Lieutenant Harold Harlamert, courtesy Linda Siemens.*

POWs at the Camp Dubois sawmill. *Photo by Lieutenant Harold Harlamert, courtesy Linda Siemens.*

this building as the camp kitchen. They sat separately but ate the same food, which was supplied by the Wyoming Tie and Timber Company.[268]

The enlisted men and prisoners had separate latrines and washroom facilities. Wooden boardwalks led to the latrines and washrooms. The camp commander described how water was heated over an open fire, carried up the washroom steps and emptied into large cans on the roof, then piped inside to shower heads so the enlisted men could take hot showers.[269] A former Camp Dubois POW told his family that the prisoners also heated water and snow for washing.[270]

Several prisoners worked at the Camp Dubois sawmill cutting firewood. During the late fall and early winter months, when the camp staff was reduced, the camp commander reported that he also chopped a lot of wood to help keep up with the increased need for firewood. POWs also worked at the camp as cooks and did maintenance work.[271]

Harlamert related details about the work involved in temporarily closing the camp during the winter and spring of 1945. He described how their equipment and property were stored in one of the large bunkhouses at the Wyoming Tie and Timber Company headquarters located eight miles from the camp. They left all the tents standing with the stoves inside. After each snow, a man was sent from the headquarters to the camp to rake snow off the tents so they would not collapse. The prisoners also braced the roofs in the kitchens so they would not collapse under the weight of heavy snow.[272] The camp was reactivated in late June 1945 and operated through the summer, fall and into early winter of 1945–46.[273]

The German POWs at Camp Dubois

During their spare time in camp, the prisoners enjoyed reading, writing, playing musical instruments and undertaking woodworking projects.[274] The Scottsbluff POW camp newspaper was provided to the prisoners at Camp Dubois. In December 1944, a check for $31.25 for POW newspaper renewal costs was documented in the camp records.[275]

The POWs also made special gifts for others. One of the camp guard's families shared a photo of a beautiful chest made and labeled by three Camp Dubois POW craftsmen as a gift for the guard's wife.[276] Some POWs also enjoyed hiking, fishing and swimming during their time off.[277]

Camp Dubois prisoners of war created a variety of literature that provides an important primary source of historical information. Their letters, essays and poems provide invaluable insight into the lives and thoughts of the prisoners. Harlamert documented some of the literary achievements of the prisoners, including a song written about Wyoming by one of the POWs.[278] Several of the poems and essays written by Camp Dubois POWs are included in the Camp Scottsbluff POW newspaper and were originally translated in an article written about German POWs in Wyoming by Bangerter in 1979.[279] The following poem was written by Rudolf Ritschel, and he made it into a song about Wyoming:

Wonderful Wyoming

How still and peaceful lies the world
Down here now, right at my feet.
You glorious mountains and steep heights too,
You quiet lakes, and green valleys' view,
O Wyoming, how fair are you!

O Wyoming, how fair are you!
My eye will ne'er tire of the view,
Many brooklets splash bright in the sun,
Over spraying, foaming waterfalls they run,
And o'er everything golden sunlight is spun.

O Wyoming, how fair you are,
When over the plains the herds wander far
And with them the cowboy upon his steed,

On free earth a free man indeed,
Who at the campfire lives and sings,
Who loves his homeland, his beautiful Wyoming.

O Wyoming, how fair are you
When the icy snowstorm hides the heights from view,
When moose and bear—by hunger annoyed—
From their loneness come
And draw near to men.
When in the hoar frost there glitter forest and hill,
And bewitched by this splendor each voice becomes still,
And my heart rejoicing sings
You wonderful fair Wyoming.[280]

Rudolf Ritschel was a German POW who worked at Camp Dubois during the summer of 1944. Through his many detailed writings, he provided important historical information about Camp Dubois, including the setting up of the camp and his life as a prisoner. Ritschel later worked and continued to write at the Camp Veteran, Wyoming POW camp in 1945. According to Ritschel, his time at Camp Dubois was "the most beautiful time" of his internment, and he would never forget the experience.[281] Ritschel shared many of memories of his time spent at Camp Dubois. He wrote about the excitement of seeing real cowboys and the large herds of cattle. Ritschel described the beautiful views of the Rocky Mountains he experienced. He said, "it was a special kind of romanticism for me to have lived up there among the loggers, cut off from the outside world." Ritschel also related how the isolation of the timber camp helped to develop friendly relationships between prisoners and guards.[282]

Corporal Fritz Hartung was a German POW at Camp Dubois who also documented and provided substantial information about Camp Dubois. Hartung had been a paratrooper in the German army before he was captured in Italy. He shared his photographs and memories with his family. Hartung said that the German POWs were provided with books on how to speak English while on the transport ships to the United States. He took the opportunity to study English so that he could learn to communicate better with others. Hartung worked in the camp kitchen and at the camp sawmills.[283]

Hartung reported that security was not strict at Camp Dubois. When he was not working, he enjoyed swimming in the lakes and hiking in the mountains. Hartung returned to Dubois and visited the former POW camp site in 1975 with his wife and daughters. They walked through the site, and he shared his memories and details of camp life, which was featured in a local newspaper article.[284]

Harlamert reported several times in his camp correspondence that logging was a dangerous industry. In 1945, a German doctor, Dr. Heinz Goebel, and a medic were assigned to the Dubois POW camp. The camp commander reported that Dr. Goebel was an excellent doctor and spoke English.[285] In addition to dealing with a prisoner death that occurred near the camp from an accident while cutting trees, other serious accidents were also reported that required medical attention. One involved a prisoner's pants being caught in a saw operated at an outlying sawmill. The prisoner was badly mangled. Another accident occurred at a nearby sawmill in which a POW almost had his thumb completely cut off. One prisoner suffered a fractured skull from a falling tree. Another prisoner broke his leg. An additional accident was caused by a prisoner jumping out of a truck and landing on an axe that was not stored properly. The prisoner cut his arm severely and required stitches.[286]

In 1945, religious services were provided to prisoners at Camp Dubois every other week on Sunday afternoons. A Lutheran minister, Reverend Frederick A. Niedner, traveled to the POW camp from the Mount Hope Lutheran Church in Kinnear, Wyoming, to conduct services for the prisoners in German. Reverend Niedner related that the young prisoners sometimes wept when they sang hymns and heard scriptures and preaching in their own language. The camp commander reported that 31 of the 138 prisoners at the camp attended the first Protestant service held at the camp in July 1945.[287]

German Officials Assist in Locating Former POW

Government officials in Germany assisted in locating a former Camp Dubois prisoner of war. In February 2017, German officials confirmed that they had located one surviving former Camp Dubois POW, Johann Pilhofer, ninety-six years old and still living in Germany. They contacted him, and he agreed to share his experiences. Written and Skype interviews were conducted by the author with Pilhofer in April 2017, with assistance from his grandson and a Dubois High School exchange student from Germany.[288]

Former Camp Dubois POW Johann Pilhofer and his grandson during a Skype interview in April 2017. *Courtesy Caleb Neale.*

Pilhofer stated that he was a prisoner of war at Camp Dubois from May 1945 into September 1945. When he left Camp Dubois, he returned to Camp Scottsbluff to assist farmers with the local crop harvests. Pilhofer provided a firsthand account of his life as a POW at Camp Dubois and at other camp locations where he worked. At Camp Dubois, he said the prisoners worked with the civilian loggers. Pilhofer described the work the prisoners did cutting down timber in the forests to make railroad ties. He said that they cut off the branches and cut the logs to specific lengths. Then they slid the logs down the mountains.[289]

Pilhofer recalled the snow that occurred in the surrounding mountains near Camp Dubois, even in the summer months, due to the high elevation of the camp. He was fascinated with the cowboys who worked in the area. He particularly remembered one cowboy who did timber work with them.[290]

According to Pilhofer, the prisoners got up at 6:00 a.m. and left the camp by 7:00 a.m. They worked in the forest all day cutting down trees. Since they worked with civilian loggers, they had both Saturdays and Sundays off to rest. Pilhofer said that they were not heavily guarded and were treated very well.[291]

Pilhofer also related how the guards shot wild game, such as deer. The prisoners helped process the game in the camp kitchen right away, because they were aware it was poaching and were told there was a penalty if they got caught. The meat was shared with the prisoners.[292]

Pilhofer reported that the prisoners did not have much free time for other activities and were too tired anyway after working so hard. He said they slept in folding beds with two blankets. Pilhofer remembered that they washed in the creek. He said the water was clean but cold. Pilhofer also related how the prisoners washed their clothes in the creek with soap on a table.[293] The prisoners used large pots and pans for washing and boiling their clothes.[294]

POWs Work on the Tie Drive in 1945

According to Harlamert's records, the Camp Dubois POWs did not assist in the local annual tie drives to Riverton. In 1945, a group of fifty prisoners, along with their own commanding officer, was brought from Camp Scottsbluff specifically for the tie drive. They were housed in tents along the river. The German POW doctor was the only Camp Dubois POW assigned to the drive. The doctor's services were needed when a prisoner on the tie drive broke his leg.[295]

Snowbound at Camp Dubois, Christmas 1944

The camp commander shared his memories of Christmas 1944, when the U.S. military personnel and POWs were all snowbound at the Dubois camp for several days with over three feet of snow. In a letter to his family, Harlamert wrote:

> *Last night I attended a program put on by the German PWs in their mess hall. It lasted for two hours. It was exceptionally good and I really enjoyed it. The PWs had their mess hall all decorated with wreathes and greenery from the forest. They built a platform for the program and had a Christmas tree with candles and even special lighting for the event.*
>
> *When we went into the mess hall the tables were all full of Christmas items including nuts, candy, cookies, cookie houses made by the PW cooks, oranges, and apples, and among all things—four bottles of beer for each PW. Beer has been pretty difficult to get up here due to it being rationed so the little beer they were able to get before Christmas they saved for the big*

Camp Dubois POW cooks with Christmas cakes in 1944. *Photo by Lieutenant Harold Harlamert, courtesy Linda Siemens.*

> *event....They invited all the American personnel to the party too and had a special table prepared for us—which included beer and candy which they paid for out of their own money.*

Harlamert related that the program included Christmas music by a small orchestra and singing led by a quintet that engaged the entire audience. The POWs enjoyed special songs, poems and writings that made fun of specific POWs and military personnel, including the camp commander. Harlamert took a photo of the POW cooks at Camp Dubois outside with their Christmas cakes in 1944.[296]

Local Residents Share Their Memories

The Camp Dubois POW timber camp was very isolated, and interaction with the local residents was limited. However, several community residents shared their memories during interviews with the author about Camp Dubois and its residents. They described the military staff who came into town for the mail, visiting the POW camp and the work that the prisoners accomplished.[297]

One especially informative interview was with Kip MacMillan, an area resident who spent the night at the POW camp as a young child. MacMillan's grandfather was Ricker Van Metre, president of the Wyoming Tie and

Timber Company. MacMillan described his visit to the Dubois POW camp with his grandfather. He remembered that one prisoner even gave up his bed so he would be more comfortable. MacMillan also recalled getting a haircut at the camp by a German barber. MacMillan acknowledged the importance of the hard work by the Camp Dubois prisoners in cutting down trees and working at the sawmills to make railroad ties, which were needed to maintain railroads during the war.[298]

Area Residents Complain About Beer for Camp Dubois POWs

Although most of the newspaper coverage reported work progress and positive achievements by the Wyoming prisoners of war, one 1944 local newspaper article raised concern about the Camp Dubois prisoners obtaining beverages that were in short supply for Wyoming residents. The newspaper reported that a truckload of beer passed through Riverton headed to the German POW camp above Dubois "to be delivered to our enemies who fought against us and were captured." In addition, it was reported that Coca-Cola, another beverage that was hard to get for American citizens, was readily available at the POW camp.[299]

Camp Dubois Site Remains

Studying, researching and interpreting the physical remains of Camp Dubois and other former POW camp sites are important aspects of the research on Wyoming World War II POW camps. After Camp Dubois closed, the structures were dismantled, and the site was cleared and bulldozed, leaving few remains of the camp structures. Based on review of military records, site plans, oral histories, written descriptions, old photographs and interpretation of remains, a well-developed record has evolved about what Camp Dubois looked like and how it operated from 1944 to 1946.[300]

There is limited evidence of the former POW camp at the site. The camp access road is in good condition. The internal camp road system can be identified, although it is overgrown with vegetation. Portions of the wood boardwalks that provided walkways between the tents and the latrines and wash areas remain intact. Small sections of the wood flumes that carried water to the mess halls and wash areas are evident. Building foundations and the remains of the springhouse are also visible at the site.[301]

TIMBER BRANCH CAMPS IN SOUTHEASTERN WYOMING MOUNTAINS

CAMP ESTERBROOK, ALBANY COUNTY

Camp Esterbrook Serves as Small Timber Camp

The Esterbrook POW camp was a small timber camp located on private land near the Laramie Peak area.[302] In the spring of 1944, twenty-five German prisoners from Camp Douglas replaced the Italian prisoners who previously had been sent to the Camp Esterbrook area to work.[303] In late June 1944, a local newspaper reported that twenty-one prisoners were working in the lumber camps in the mountains south of Douglas.[304] After Camp Douglas was reactivated in August 1944, a larger work crew of approximately seventy-five prisoners returned to work at Camp Esterbrook.[305]

The prisoners worked cutting timber in the Laramie Peak area for Douglas lumbermen F.W. "Floyd" Bartling and Tony Funk. Bartling and Funk also employed eight Italian prisoners to work at their post plant in Douglas. According to Bartling, the POW timber crew was sent to Esterbrook accompanied by six guards. However, the guards seldom went into the woods with the prisoners. The prisoners never tried to escape. Bartling said they "seemed to appreciate the privilege of spending time in the mountains."[306]

The buildings and structures were removed from the site, but evidence of the former POW camp exists. Two rectangular concrete foundations depict the location of the POW camp buildings. In addition, remains of the well structure and the latrine pit area are visible.[307]

Camp Esterbrook foundations indicate the location of POW camp buildings. *Author's collection.*

Camp Centennial barracks at former CCC camp housed the prisoners of war in 1945. *Nici Self Historical Museum, Centennial.*

CENTENNIAL POW CAMP, ALBANY COUNTY

Camp Centennial Operates in 1945

The Centennial POW camp operated only during 1945. According to a local newspaper report, six truckloads of prisoners were transported to the camp at the end of July. The camp was located at the former CCC camp at Mullen Creek near Centennial. The CCC camp was converted into an Army Air Forces rest camp in 1943 and operated during the war, into the summer of 1945. During the summer, the camp was again modified to serve as a prisoner of war camp to house approximately 150 to 200 German POWs.[308]

The prisoners were housed in the former CCC camp buildings. There was a seven- to eight-foot-high square wire fence with razor wire on top around the camp. There were armed guards stationed at the POW camp.[309]

The prisoners were employed by the Wyoming Timber Company for timber work. They worked in the forest cutting down trees.[310] The prisoners from the Centennial POW camp cut approximately two million board feet of timber in the Medicine Bow National Forest by mid-November 1945.[311]

RYAN PARK POW CAMP, CARBON COUNTY

The Italian Prisoners Arrive

The Ryan Park POW camp was a timber camp established in late October 1943.[312] The prisoners were housed at the former Ryan Park CCC camp. The prisoner of war labor was requested by R.R. Crow & Company to harvest timber in the Medicine Bow National Forest because of the difficulty obtaining other labor sources during the war.[313]

The first group of 114 Italian prisoners arrived at the Ryan Park camp on October 24, 1943, from Camp Douglas. The prisoners worked at cutting, skidding and other logging activities.[314] During the first fall and winter of operation (1943–44), approximately 200 Italian prisoners worked from the camp producing railroad ties and mine props.[315]

A local newspaper reported that Reverend D.N. Shotwell visited the camp in November 1943. The reverend appealed for help from local people to provide items for the Italian prisoners, to show some "good neighbor spirit." Articles requested included Italian–English dictionaries, Italian classical sheet music, a piano, phonograph records, Italian periodicals and games.[316]

Meryle Hansen Shares Information about POW Camp Life and Work

Seven R.R. Crow & Company instructors worked with the POWs, training them in timber harvest methods. Meryle Hansen was one of the POW instructors. Hansen provided detailed information about the Ryan Park POW camp and the work the prisoners did. Oral history tapes of interviews with Hansen were transcribed and are included in the Wyoming State Archives.[317]

In addition, Hansen made a sketch of the Ryan Park camp based on his memories of the camp, donating it to the Brush Creek Ranger District, USDA Forest Service, Medicine Bow National Forest.[318] Hansen later worked as a volunteer for the U.S. Forest Service at the Ryan Park Campground. Hansen provided visitors with firsthand information and stories about the former POW camp site and prisoners.[319]

According to Hansen, the Italian prisoners enjoyed singing, dancing, painting, drawing, woodworking and acrobatics. Several of the instructors pooled some money to buy musical instruments so they could form a small band. The prisoners sang, danced and played for the instructors and their families on Saturday afternoons. Hansen described the prisoners as trustworthy and very knowledgeable, but they "didn't care much about work."[320]

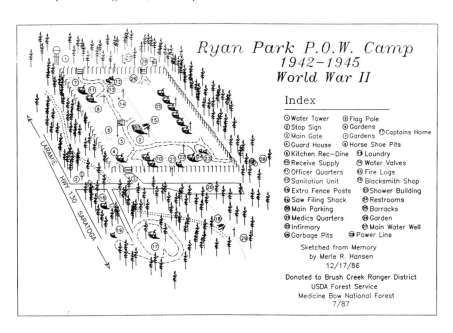

Ryan Park POW camp map sketched by Meryle Hansen. *Carbon County Museum.*

Painting by Ryan Park Austrian POW Josef Szirola of a winter scene on a marble box lid. *Wyoming State Museum, Department of State Parks and Cultural Resources.*

Hand-carved trinket box by Ryan Park POW Josef Szirola with a forest scene painted on the inside lid. *Wyoming State Museum, Department of State Parks and Cultural Resources.*

On April 11, 1944, the Italian prisoners were returned to Camp Douglas, due to the change in status of the Italian prisoners of war.[321] Mr. R.R. Crow reported that the work performed by the Italian prisoners was "very satisfactory." He stated that the "operation of the mill would have been severely curtailed" without the POW labor.[322]

German POWs Replace the Italian Prisoners

In 1944, approximately three hundred German and Austrian prisoners were assigned to the Ryan Park POW camp.[323] During the summer, prisoners were supplied from the Greeley, Colorado POW camp.[324] Hansen related that the two groups did not get along well and camp staff sometimes had problems with some of the prisoners, including riots. The "troublemakers" were identified and sent back to Camp Douglas for replacement workers.[325]

Hansen said that the German prisoners liked to work on the camp flowerbeds and gardens. They also built a water wheel and carved wood figures that were about two feet tall. The water wheel powered the animated figures to do activities such as "cut wood, saw wood, and wash clothes." The prisoners also enjoyed playing horseshoes at the camp. Hansen returned to the former POW camp site in November 1988 to formally document his memories. He pointed out the extent of the horseshoe court and noted that one of the horseshoe stakes was still standing in place at the site.[326]

Hansen described in detail the work the prisoners did in the forest. They left the camp in the mornings by 6:30 a.m. They worked in the high country timber areas. One of the camps was in the North Brush Creek area, located at a high elevation, about ten thousand feet. The high altitude bothered some of the prisoners, but they adapted. Hansen reported that both the Italian and German prisoners had their own paramedics to handle injuries and illnesses at the camp. An interpreter and a guard also accompanied the prisoners. Hansen reported that the prisoners were served a hot lunch, although he packed a cold bag lunch. They returned to the camp about 5:00 p.m.[327]

Hansen marked the trees to be cut by the prisoners in the forest. Job-training sheets giving step-by-step directions for cutting down trees and building the skidway and trails were provided in both German and English.[328] Hansen related that when the snow got too deep, the prisoners had to shovel out the base of the tree before it was cut. This added to their work, but there were specific rules pertaining to the height of the remaining tree stumps.[329]

Although most of the prisoners were cooperative, Hansen recalled one incident in which he acknowledged the potential hazards of the job and the importance of the quick action of the guard who was present. Hansen related that he had just shown the prisoners how high to cut the trees above the ground when a young German POW ran up behind him with a double-bit axe raised. The armed guard warned the prisoner "that he was in his sights" and to drop the axe. That group of prisoners was returned to the base camp and replaced with a "really good bunch."[330]

Local Residents Share Information and Memories About the Prisoners

Art Bergquist, a Saratoga resident, was a tie inspector for the Union Pacific Railroad and worked with some of the Ryan Park prisoners. One of the POWs, Gottard Henning, gave Bergquist a photograph of a group of German POWs who worked at Ryan Park. Bergquist and Henning corresponded with each other after the war. Bergquist sent the former POW care packages. Bergquist donated the POW photo to the Carbon County Museum.[331]

Ryan Park German POW timber crew, with one POW officer in back row wearing uniform. *Carbon County Museum.*

Local resident Neal Ward remembered stories his father told him about the POWs and the work they did. His father, Fred Ward Sr., worked at one of the horse barns on Brush Creek. The prisoners helped him with caring for the horses, harness repair and horse shoeing. His father told him the prisoners were excellent at shoeing horses.

Several years after the war, Ward met a man visiting the area who asked him if he knew much about the old Ryan Park POW camp. They discussed the camp, and the man told Ward he was a former U.S. Army officer. His responsibilities included checking German POWs to identify "SS personnel." Each prisoner's armpits were inspected to see if they had a tattoo with three small dots in a triangle, which indicated membership in the SS. Ward related that the former officer identified two "SS soldiers" at the Ryan Park POW camp. They were removed from the camp.[332]

An Escape from Ryan Park

In July 1944, four Camp Ryan Park German prisoners escaped from their work site while cutting trees. They were recaptured a few days later sitting in the bleachers at the rodeo grounds in Saratoga.[333] According to Meyrle Hansen, this was the only escape from camp work at Ryan Park. Hansen said the prisoners were given a second chance and never left again. He recalled the prisoners had "sore feet, their faces were burnt" and they had blisters on their lips when they were found.[334]

Local Historian Keeps Ryan Park POW Camp History Alive

Local historian Dick Perue has conducted research and compiled information about the Ryan Park POW camp over the past several years. At recent public slide show presentations by Perue about the camp, a summer resident of Ryan Park informed him that she lives in one of the former buildings that had been moved from the POW camp to the nearby community of Ryan Park in the 1950s. She said that the prisoners created pencil drawings on the building walls as well as framed drawings. She provided Perue with photos of a framed colored pencil drawing found in her cabin of a meadow village scene with a windmill and cows grazing. The drawing is signed by "P.O.W. Riboni Renio, Italy" and dated November 1943.[335]

Former Ryan Park POW Returns to the United States to Live

A local newspaper reported that Otto Wietasch, a former Ryan Park POW, returned to the former camp site in Wyoming to visit in 1979. Wietasch worked as a prisoner of war cutting timber and railroad ties near the Ryan Park POW camp for two years. After the war, Wietasch returned to the United States with his family and lived in Amity, Pennsylvania, where he owned and operated a grocery store. Wietasch and his family became U.S. citizens in 1964.[336]

The Ryan Park POW Camp Site Today

The U.S. Forest Service operates the Ryan Park Campground at the former Ryan Park POW camp site. An interpretive sign at the entrance to the campground provides information about the Ryan Park POW and CCC camps. In addition, an interpretive trail with numbered posts through the former POW camp site identifies the location of some of the buildings and describes details of camp life.[337]

7

AGRICULTURAL BRANCH CAMPS IN SOUTHEASTERN WYOMING

CAMP WHEATLAND, PLATTE COUNTY

Camp Wheatland Operates at the Fairgrounds

In 1943, prisoners were transported to and from Camp Douglas daily to work on farms in the Wheatland area. Approximately fifty Italian POWs assisted farmers with the local beet harvest in the fall. They worked six and a half hours a day and were divided into four groups; two guards were assigned to each group of prisoners.[338]

In 1944, a prisoner of war camp at Wheatland was established. Camp Wheatland was located at the Platte County Fairgrounds site. Modifications to the fairgrounds for the operation of the POW camp included the installation of a fence enclosing the restricted area of the camp. In addition, a mess hall and a bathhouse were constructed for use by the prisoners. The POWs worked a ten-hour day. They were paid prevailing county wages. The camp was designed to house up to 250 prisoners of war.[339]

There were separate mess halls and latrines for the U.S. Army enlisted men and prisoners of war. In addition to the tents utilized for housing the POWs, three granary buildings were used as barracks for the prisoners. The camp commander and camp headquarters were also housed in tents.[340]

Camp Wheatland at the Platte County Fairgrounds showing tents used by both prisoners and U.S. military personnel in June 1945. *Laramie Peak Museum, Wheatland, Wyoming, courtesy Judy Wilson.*

Prisoner Work at Camp Wheatland

A local newspaper reported that the first group of 100 war prisoners was scheduled to arrive the second week of May 1944 from Camp Douglas to work in the area beet fields; however, they arrived a few weeks later.[341] During June 1944, 100 German POWs were sent to Camp Wheatland to work for about six weeks in the beet fields. Then, from early October into November, approximately 160 German POWs were sent to work during the beet harvest. They were sent back to the Camp Scottsbluff base camp in November after the harvest was completed.[342]

During the summer of 1944, two German prisoners escaped briefly from Camp Wheatland. They crawled through the compound fence. The prisoners were promptly recaptured as they attempted to obtain a ride out of town.[343]

In 1945, from June into the fall, up to 250 prisoners were sent to Camp Wheatland from Camp Douglas. The prisoners worked on local farms in the hay, bean and corn fields throughout the summer. During the fall, they worked on area farms until the beet harvest was completed.[344]

Camp Wheatland POWs working in beet fields in June 1945. *Laramie Peak Museum, Wheatland, Wyoming, courtesy Judy Wilson.*

Local Residents Share Their Memories

Local resident Denzil Cochran related that his parents had German prisoners of war working on their farm in the beet fields. Cochran said that his dad would go to the fairgrounds every morning to pick the prisoners up and return them each night. He said the prisoners were housed in tents. His mother would cook up a batch of beans for them. Cochran would take the beans out to the prisoners at lunchtime. Cochran said they really seemed to enjoy the extra food.[345]

Ron Wilhelm remembered his dad, John Wilhelm, taking the beet truck to the POW camp in Wheatland to pick up prisoners, too. His father picked up between two and twelve prisoners, depending on the work he needed done. The prisoners thinned and weeded the beets in the summer. Then, in the fall, the POWs helped with the harvest. The prisoners topped the beets by hand. Wilhelm recalled that there was one prisoner who "got very handy" operating his father's tractor and that his dad trusted him with it. Wilhelm said the prisoners were "very good help" to his father and other area farmers.[346]

POWs were transported from the Wheatland camp to John Wilhelm's farm in his beet truck. *Courtesy Ron Wilhelm.*

After they got better acquainted with the prisoners, Wilhelm's mother noticed what the men were provided to eat in the lunches sent from the camp. Wilhelm's parents had a big apple orchard on their farm. His mother made baked apples in the bunkhouse cookstove oven for the prisoners. Wilhelm said the POWs were very pleased to have the baked apples as a change from the food they were provided with by the army.[347]

Wilhelm related that one prisoner built a small wood box for his mother. He said it was simple "but attractive with inlaid designs" that included a horseshoe and a four-leaf clover. Another former Camp Wheatland prisoner was a jeweler in Germany. After he returned to Germany, he made Wilhelm's mother a jewelry box and sent it to her.[348]

Wilhelm said that many of the prisoners wanted to go to church. On Sunday mornings, church services were provided in German to the prisoners at the Evangelical Bethlehem Church in Wheatland. The services for the prisoners were held early in the morning, before the regular congregation services. Wilhelm remembered watching and listening to the prisoners as they marched to the church, approximately one and a half miles from the camp, singing in German all the way. Wilhelm recalled that there were mixed emotions within the community about providing church services for the German prisoners, who were considered our enemy.[349]

The buildings used as the prisoner of war mess hall and latrines still stand at the fairgrounds. The former mess hall is currently used as an exhibit hall. The original fireplace in the building still exists. Murals painted on the sides of the former mess hall building by area artists depict local historic scenes. The former latrine building continued to be utilized for restrooms at the fairgrounds through the summer of 2017.[350]

GOSHEN COUNTY POW CAMPS AND PRISONERS

Goshen County, Wyoming, hosted four prisoner of war camps, at Veteran, Torrington, Lingle and Huntley. Camp Veteran operated the longest, from late September 1943 into January 1946. Camp Torrington operated seasonally from June 1944 into November 1945. The Lingle and Huntley POW camps operated only in 1945. Prisoners assigned to the Goshen County POW camps worked primarily in the beet, potato and bean fields.[351]

The four Goshen County POW camps supplied 1,150 prisoners to assist with the 1945 sugar beet harvest. The Goshen County Labor Association reported that the prisoner of war labor and other labor available would be "just barely adequate" to harvest the beet crop, which was expected to be "one of the largest bumper crop of beets in many years." A local newspaper reported that the number of prisoners allocated for each camp was 300 for Camp Lingle, 400 for Camp Torrington, 300 for Camp Veteran and 150 at Camp Huntley.[352]

Temporary Use of Armory

In October 1944, the state farm labor committee met in Torrington and recognized the need for additional prisoner labor to complete the beet harvest in Goshen County and secured additional prisoners to save the beet crop. According to a local newspaper report, coordination between the Goshen County Labor Association, extension service representatives and Camp Scottsbluff officials resulted in temporary housing facilities being constructed at the armory for two hundred prisoners of war. Field kitchens, portable showers and supervisory personnel were supplied by Fort F.E. Warren. Sixteen local farmers donated their services to build a fence and make other necessary modifications for housing the prisoners.[353]

American Legion against Local Farmers Feeding Prisoners

At the annual meeting of the Goshen County Labor Association in late February 1944, Major Richard Parnell, from the Scottsbluff POW base camp, spoke to local farmers. He warned them against providing the prisoners with any additional food or special favors. He told the farmers that the prisoners were well fed by the army and received the same food U.S. soldiers were provided with.[354] In September 1945, both the Torrington and Veteran American Legion posts passed resolutions protesting the additional food fed to prisoners by Goshen County farmers.[355]

Proposed POW Labor Plan Is Opposed by American Legion

In 1945, the Goshen County Beet Growers Association proposed a POW Labor Plan that provided for prisoners to be "farmed out" on a parole system and housed directly on local farms to work. The beet farmers asserted that the change in the current system, which required that prisoners live in prison side camps and be accompanied by a guard, would improve results in the fieldwork done by the prisoners. The beet growers pointed out that in England, German prisoners of war were farmed out on a parole system without guards.[356]

The Veteran American Legion strongly opposed the new proposed labor plan, based on their belief that a parole system for POWs would be dangerous to the community and the nation, could cause potential problems between the citizens and POWs, would be "un-American" and that the existing system worked satisfactorily.[357]

CAMP TORRINGTON, GOSHEN COUNTY

Camp Torrington Operates in 1944 and 1945

The Torrington prisoner of war camp operated seasonally from June 1944 through the end of the potato and beet harvests in November 1945.[358] Camp Torrington was located south of the Holly Sugar Beet Factory.[359] The prisoners were sent from Camp Scottsbluff and worked primarily on local farms in the sugar beet, potato and bean fields.[360]

In 1944, prisoners from Camp Torrington were also sent to work in Huntley at the Jones Potato Warehouse, owned by Charley Jones. According to Beverly (Jones) Babcock, she was about thirteen years old when she worked at the potato warehouse with the Italian prisoners. Babcock remembered that the prisoners were polite and cordial. One prisoner was a violinist, and several were professional men. The prisoners washed, sorted and bagged potatoes and loaded them into railroad cars.[361]

Two Prisoners Escape from Camp Torrington

Two prisoners escaped from the Torrington POW camp on October 2, 1944, but were captured the same day a few miles from camp. A local newspaper reported that the prisoners believed that they were crossing the border into Mexico, because they had reached the dry-land farming area beyond the irrigated fields. The young prisoners, who were eighteen and twenty-three years old, "surrendered peacefully at a local farmhouse." The prisoners were returned to Camp Scottsbluff to face disciplinary action.[362]

Camp Torrington Prisoners Assist Local Farmers

Shirley Heckart remembered her father, Kelvie "Butch" Beers, talking about the prisoners who worked on Shorty Bath's farm. Her father and uncle worked with a German POW, who had been a butcher, at Neal Wilhite's slaughterhouse. Heckart's mother was upset because the prisoner worked with knives alongside the other men, but her father trusted him. Heckart recalled driving by the POW camp. Her father would stop the car, get out and whistle loudly to the prisoners. Then, he would throw cigarettes over the fence to them.[363]

Former POW Paul Stutz reported that he arrived at Camp Scottsbluff in May 1945 and was then sent to Camp Torrington with a group of about three hundred German prisoners. At Camp Torrington, the prisoners were separated into groups based on political party affiliation; Stutz was sent to Camp Veteran.[364] By June 1945, both the Torrington and Veteran camps were filled with several hundred prisoners of war. In September, the prisoners worked primarily harvesting potatoes and beans. Approximately four hundred prisoners of war were housed at Camp Torrington in October to assist local farmers with harvesting sugar beets.[365]

CAMP VETERAN, GOSHEN COUNTY

Camp Veteran Operates from 1943 to 1946

Camp Veteran operated from late September 1943 into January 1946 after a contract was signed by the Goshen County Beet Growers Association and the War Department on August 16, 1943.[366] The prisoners worked primarily in the bean, potato and sugar beet fields. The prisoners were housed at the former Veteran CCC camp site that had been modified to accommodate up to 270 prisoners supplied from Camp Scottsbluff.[367] Renovations were made to the CCC camp, including the installation of a seven-and-a-half-foot-high fence around the camp. Many prisoners remained at the Camp Veteran branch camp rather than being returned to Camp Scottsbluff, even after the fall harvests in 1944 and 1945 were completed.[368]

Camp Veteran Prisoners

The prisoners could be employed hourly or piece rate in any type of farmwork. Farmers submitted applications for their employment through the Goshen County Agent's office. The prisoners were picked up from the camp by local farmers between 7:30 and 8:00 a.m. to work on area farms and had to be returned to the camp by 5:30 p.m.[369]

Some of the prisoners at Camp Veteran were very young. One prisoner was a boy who was fourteen or fifteen years old. A medical doctor was also assigned to the POW camp at Veteran.[370]

According to former Camp Veteran POW Walter Kurcon, there were 250 prisoners at the camp when he arrived in August 1944. That number included "Austrians, Germans, Frances, Slovians, and two Italians." Kurcon recalled that, at first, Camp Veteran was a disappointment to him. He noted the old barracks and "few comforts." However, Kurcon said that they experienced "some freedoms, silence and a kind of coziness." He indicated they had no disputes or problems. He related that he celebrated Christmas Eve 1945 and "a Happy New Year 1946" at the Veteran POW camp.[371]

The Veteran POW camp utilized the former Veteran CCC camp site and barracks. *Wyoming State Archives*.

Camp Veteran YMCA Reports

YMCA reports by Dr. Harold Hong describe religious, educational and recreational activities at Camp Veteran observed during his inspection on December 18, 1944. Dr. Hong reported that religious services were provided by a local Catholic priest and that a Lutheran pastor offered to provide services to Protestants. Materials for services were supplied by the YMCA, the local priest and the Lutheran Commission for Prisoners of War. Dr. Hong indicated that a building outside the stockade was designated for use by religious groups. He noted the increases in classes available in the winter compared to the summer, due to the seasonal needs of prisoner labor. Classes in painting and foreign languages were the best attended. Dr. Hong reported that the camp library was slowly being built up. Eight languages were spoken at the camp. Musical activities and theatrical presentations were available. The musical groups were gearing up for upcoming Christmas festivities during his visit. Hong noted that painting and wood carving were very popular activities at the camp.[372]

POWs Share Their Experiences at Camp Veteran

POW Rudolf Ritschel described his experiences of the time he spent in Camp Veteran in 1945. He reported that the "facilities were very primitive, but a good spirit of comradeship prevailed." Ritschel shared memories of the prisoners' efforts to relieve the monotony of camp life. He said that the prisoners were "artists, painters and sculptors" and created works with primitive tools and materials. In addition, the prisoners wrote plays and presented a variety of performances, which even resulted in officers traveling from Camp Scottsbluff to see a show.[373]

Paul Stutz, a former POW at Camp Veteran, also provided details of his internment in an interview conducted by Wyoming State Museum staff in 1993. Stutz returned to Goshen County to visit a family he had made friends with during the war. Stutz stated that he was sixteen and a half years old when he joined the German army in 1944. He was captured and arrived in the United States on May 7, 1945. The prisoners were told the next day by an American officer that the war was over and they would be going home soon. However, the prisoners were sent to Camp Scottsbluff. He was then sent to Camp Torrington, where the prisoners who had no party ties to National Socialism such as Stutz, were assigned to Camp Veteran. According to Stutz, there were only German and Austrian prisoners at the camp at that time.[374]

Stutz reported how the prisoners were assigned to several different farms. They did not go to the same farm every day, so they couldn't make friends. They were not allowed to speak with the American officers or local farm people. The farmers provided them with water. They worked eight hours daily on the farms. It was very hot, so they drank a lot of water. Some farmers did feed the prisoners, but it was very difficult to get assigned to a "good" farm, because some of the German prisoners had connections with the people in the camp office and always asked to be sent to those specific farms. The other prisoners had to work at other, less-favored farms.[375]

Positive memories shared by Stutz include meeting a Camp Veteran POW German minister who became the camp minister. They formed a Christian support group. Stutz said that the experience and the Christian foundation guided him throughout his life. Another positive memory he shared was the experience of being free, even in captivity. Stutz said he was "no longer so much under control." He stated that he "always looked for the good" wherever he was and whatever happened.[376]

According to Stutz, his worst memories were of the time he spent at Camp Veteran in the fall and winter of 1945–46, when there was no work for the prisoners. They were very bored and spent their time reading, sleeping and walking around the camp. Stutz took the opportunity to complete an English-language course during that time. He also reported that the prisoners were not allowed to send letters home from Camp Veteran. He stated that he had been allowed to submit a card with only twenty-five words and his camp address so that his family would know where he was and that he was alive.[377]

David Eddington points out the Camp Veteran walkway remains to the author. *Author's collection.*

Stutz related that the POWs left at the end of January 1946 and were transported by an army troopship to Great Britain. They were told they would be there for two months and were turned over by American officers to the British. However, they kept him in England to work for two more years.[378]

According to Stutz, he was finally dismissed from England on June 3, 1948, and returned home. He turned twenty-one years old a few weeks later. Stutz commented on "the lack of justice" that he was recognized as having "nothing to do with National Socialism" and was sent to England in the spring of 1946 for two additional years. However, the prisoners identified as "Party Members" at Scottsbluff were sent home in the fall of 1946.[379]

Area resident David Eddington recalled the operation of both the POW and CCC camps at Veteran. He stayed overnight in the kitchen with friends in 1938, when it was a CCC camp. Eddington's farm and the POW camp shared a common boundary corner. Eddington identified the specific buildings that existed on the site of the former CCC/POW camp shown on a photograph and provided details about their use. The buildings included the headquarters (or Administration Office), a kitchen-dining building, infirmary, showers and restrooms, truck garages, a storage building for oil and grease supplies and a blacksmith shop. Eddington bought the blacksmith shop that was used at the former camp site for twenty-five dollars and moved it to his farm after the war. He related how the prisoners used to love to run the tractors. Today, remains of concrete sidewalks and foundations help to indicate the location of the barracks and other buildings and structures used at the former POW camp site.[380]

CAMP LINGLE, GOSHEN COUNTY

Camp Lingle Operates in 1945

Camp Lingle operated from June 1945 into the last week of November 1945.[381] Approximately three hundred prisoners were sent from the Camp Scottsbluff POW base camp to work on local farms. Camp Lingle was located west of Lingle, adjacent to Highway 26, on property owned by the Holly Sugar Corporation.[382]

In mid-March 1945, work started on preparing buildings for the new POW camp, which was built to help alleviate transporting prisoners long distances to Lingle-area farms.[383] The sugar company dormitories were modified to accommodate the war prisoners. The camp construction was completed by early June to house the prisoners.[384]

The small building that still exists on the former POW camp site was used as a camp headquarters and housing for the POW camp guards.[385] The building was made of large red-clay brick and had green shutters that closed. The building is now covered with stucco and is currently used for apartments. Evidence of the original brick on one side of the building can still be seen.[386]

Local Residents Provide Details About Prisoners

Several local residents shared their memories about the Lingle camp, the prisoners and details of the work they did. Lingle residents reported that the prisoners were friendly and had an excellent work ethic. The prisoners worked in the fields thinning and hoeing beets, stacking hay and helping with the potato and beet harvests.[387] Most of the fieldwork was done by hand. The prisoners and guards were transported to area farms by the local farmers to work in the fields. Farmers were told not to speak with the prisoners, but many did.[388] Local farmers fed the prisoners well to supplement the lunches

Lingle POW camp headquarters and housing for the camp guards, showing evidence of the original brick wall visible on one side of the building. *Author's collection.*

the POWs brought from the camp. One farm family provided additional food, such as "fried chicken, homemade bread, cakes, watermelon and Kool-Aid" for the prisoners and took it out to the fields for their lunch.[389]

Some local farmers brought the prisoners to their homes for Sunday meals. Ruthanne (Hill) Hansen's father, Jake Hill, spoke German and served as an interpreter between the prisoners and guards. She recalled that one day her father brought five or six prisoners to their house in town for dinner. They got to know them and "got along fine." One prisoner made a suitcase for them out of a light-colored wood. Her family used it for a long time. Hansen related that when she was a sophomore in high school, part of the freshman initiation was to march the freshmen students out of town past the POW camp. She remembered the prisoners watching them march by through the fence that surrounded their camp.[390]

Lingle residents reported that they didn't have any problems with the prisoners. One resident recalled that she could sometimes hear the prisoners singing at night at the Lingle camp.[391] Some former prisoners returned to the Lingle area to visit after the war.[392]

The Lingle POW camp closed in the last week of November 1945. The prisoners were returned to the Camp Douglas POW base camp to prepare to leave the United States. A local newspaper article acknowledged that "much needed work was accomplished by the POWs throughout the war years."[393]

CAMP HUNTLEY, GOSHEN COUNTY

Camp Huntley Operates During Fall 1945

In late September 1945, a temporary POW camp was constructed about two miles southeast of Huntley on the Harold Lippincott farm. The camp operated into late November 1945 and housed approximately 150 German prisoners from Camp Scottsbluff. The POWs worked on the local farms, primarily picking potatoes and harvesting beets.[394]

The Huntley POW Camp

The camp was built by the prisoners on about three acres of land and included a tent area, a mess hall, a sixteen-foot-square shower building and the guards' quarters. The prisoners slept in sixteen-foot-square tents, eight men to a tent. The tent area that housed the prisoners was located within the compound and surrounded by a fence, but the gate was usually left open during the day. Prisoners used fifty-gallon barrels for their stoves and burned coal and wood. The mess hall was constructed on a concrete slab with Celatex siding and covered with a big tent over the top. The guards slept in the labor house, which still stands on the site.[395]

Camp Huntley Prisoners

Larry Lippincott was a young child when the prison camp was located on his father's farm. He remembered that one of the prisoners gave him a pillow that he made at the POW camp. One side was canvas, and it was filled with broom bristles.[396]

Local farmers daily transported the prisoners they needed to work on their farms to and from the camp. The farmers often supplemented the POWs' army rations. The prisoners were well fed by the Lippincott family. Lippincott's grandmother and grandfather both spoke German, so they could communicate well with the prisoners. Lippincott said that "some of the prisoners cried when they left the camp."[397]

Camp Huntley POW tents on the Lippincott farm. *Homesteaders Museum, Torrington, Wyoming.*

The former Camp Huntley guardhouse is still in use on the Lippincott family farm. *Author's collection.*

CAMP PINE BLUFFS, LARAMIE COUNTY

Pine Bluffs POW Camp Operates from 1943 to 1945

Camp Pine Bluffs operated seasonally from September 1943 into November 1945. In early September 1943, the War Department's Seventh Service Command approved a contract with the Laramie County Cooperative Producers Association to provide ninety Italian prisoners from Camp Scottsbluff to assist with the potato, bean and sugar beet harvests. A POW camp was established at the Laramie County fairgrounds in Pine Bluffs. Modifications to the fairgrounds and buildings were made to provide living quarters and food and sanitary facilities for the prisoners. In addition, a fence was installed around the POW camp. The camp staff included administrative officials, guards and cooks.[398]

The prisoners worked for growers in the Pine Bluffs and Albin areas. They were returned to the Scottsbluff POW camp after the completion of the potato and beet crop harvests in early November 1943. Local growers reported that "the prisoners were a great help in getting the beet and potato crops harvested."[399]

On September 23, 1944, 165 German prisoners were sent back to Camp Pine Bluffs from Camp Scottsbluff to work during the potato and beet harvests.[400] The sugar beet harvest was completed on November 3, 1944. The POW camp closed shortly after, and the prisoners returned to Camp Scottsbluff.[401]

In September 1945, the Pine Bluffs POW camp reopened. The local newspaper reported the harvest "of one of the largest potato crops ever grown" in the area. Most of the larger growers in the area employed German prisoners from the Pine Bluffs camp.[402] In early October 1945, the Pine Bluffs POW camp commander warned local farmers who would need POW labor to contact the camp several days in advance to make sure the prisoners would be available. Camp Pine Bluffs closed after the potato and sugar beet harvests were completed.[403]

Local Doctor Treats POWs at Camp

Pine Bluffs physician Dr. Martin Luther Morris ("Doc" Morris) served as the POW camp doctor. He developed a rapport with the prisoners—except one, whom he described as "a die-hard Nazi." The prisoner was a former prison guard in Germany. A heated argument occurred when Doc Morris prepared to lance a boil on the prisoner's back that was believed to be related to events that the prisoner witnessed when he served as a prison guard.[404]

Local Residents Provide Details of POW Work

Several local residents in the Pine Bluffs area shared memories about the POW camp and the work the prisoners did. Jack Harrison remembered when the Italian prisoners came to the Pine Bluffs POW Camp to work in the potato and sugar beet fields. Harrison said that most of the local people needed the prisoner labor badly. There was no malice toward them. According to Harrison, the prisoners were well fed and treated well.[405]

Former Albin resident Don Strube remembered the prisoners working on his parents' farm in 1943, 1944 and 1945. His father picked up the prisoners from the Pine Bluffs POW camp in his grain truck and returned them to the camp after work each day. There were about twenty prisoners, with one guard assigned. The prisoners picked potatoes. They wore belts with attached potato sacks and walked down the rows and filled the fifty-pound potato bags.[406]

In addition to the agricultural work they did in Albin, the prisoners dug ditches and assisted with hand and trim work on an addition to the Strube house. They communicated with Strube's grandfather, who spoke German.

Camp Pine Bluffs building that housed the prisoners at the former fairgrounds. *Author's collection.*

His family did not have any problems with the prisoners. Strube said that they were willing workers who did what they had to do.[407]

Pine Bluffs resident Norman Sanders helped his father, who had a freight delivery service, deliver groceries to the Pine Bluffs POW camp. All freight came into the freight dock by train. Sanders particularly remembered the crates of oranges they bought for the prisoners, because he was given an orange after each delivery.[408]

Richard Gardner remembered that his father drove to the Pine Bluffs camp to transport ten German prisoners, with one guard, to work on his farm in Kimball, Nebraska. They picked potatoes and topped beets. His mother cooked a meal for them and would warm it up for their lunch. Gardner said his father had to return the prisoners to the camp by a specific time and that the camp was strict on the rules. Gardner described the prisoners as "happy go lucky."[409]

The large building that housed the prisoners of war still stands on the former fairgrounds and POW camp site. Several changes to the building have been made over the years. Modifications include the replacement of wood siding and shingles and the installation of a new metal roof.[410]

PART III

POSTWAR WYOMING POW CAMPS AND PRISONERS

8

POSTWAR DEACTIVATION OF CAMPS AND POW LIFE

WYOMING POW CAMPS AND PRISONERS AFTER THE WAR

The Wyoming prisoner of war camps remained in operation after World War II ended officially on September 2, 1945, with the formal surrender by Japan. There were some changes in the operation of the camps, especially after the war in Europe ended on May 8, 1945. Shortly after V-E Day, prisoners experienced significant changes in the food they were served in the camps. A new food conservation policy had been recently implemented that included reductions in rations of meat and meat-type substitutions. Other food items in short supply, such as canned fruits, sugar and fats, were also reduced. Margarine was used instead of butter, and beef was provided only twice a month. In September 1945 correspondence, the camp commander at Camp Dubois reported that the prisoners did not receive any beef or pork in their rations and very little other meat. The prisoners resorted to trapping animals, such as snowshoe hares and porcupines, at the timber camp to supplement their food supply. The POW camps continued to operate to complete vital agricultural and timber work and as part of the transition period while plans for repatriation were developed. Repatriation plans involved several challenges, which included the logistics of shipping the large number of prisoners of war back to their home countries and consideration of obligations to European countries to provide prisoner labor for postwar reconstruction.[411]

Many of the Wyoming branch camps closed in late 1945 after the agricultural harvests were completed and prisoners were returned to base camps to prepare for repatriation. However, some Wyoming branch camps, including Camp Veteran and Camp Dubois, operated into early 1946.[412] The Camp Douglas base camp closed in early February 1946.[413] The Camp Scottsbluff, Nebraska base camp closed in mid-March 1946.[414] The Fort Francis E. Warren POW camp was deactivated in late April 1946.[415]

REPATRIATION OF WYOMING POWS AND LONG JOURNEYS HOME

The War Department announced that the prisoners of war would be released from private contract work by the end of February 1946 and from military work by the end of March 1946.[416] Prisoners were shipped from base camps at Camp Douglas and Camp Scottsbluff, Nebraska, starting in January 1946.[417] On July 23, 1946, the army announced that the last prisoners of war had left the United States.[418]

However, not all prisoners of war were immediately returned to their homes. In June 1945, the United States agreed to supply prisoner of war labor to help rebuild war-torn countries in Europe. After arriving in Europe, thousands of POWs were sent to Great Britain, France and other countries for several months—in many cases, years—to help in the postwar reconstruction, including former Wyoming prisoners. In an interview with former Camp Dubois POW Johann Pilhofer, he described his long journey to arrive back in Germany. Pilhofer was sent to France and England to work after he left the United States in January 1946. He returned to his home in Germany in May 1947.[419] Paul Stutz, former Camp Veteran POW, reported that he returned home on June 8, 1948, after leaving the United States at the end of January 1946 and spending over two additional years working in England.[420] Gerhard Arlt, former Camp Fort Warren German prisoner of war, left Wyoming in November 1945 and was told they were being sent home. However, he was sent to Le Havre, France, where he worked at hard labor in the mines for three years before finally returning to Germany in December 1948.[421]

FORMER WYOMING PRISONERS OF WAR
RETURN TO THE UNITED STATES

After the war, several former Wyoming POWs returned to visit the communities and POW camp sites where they had worked as prisoners. Several stories about their postwar visits are documented in local newspaper articles and in interviews with family members and local residents. Former POWs who returned to visit Wyoming include Wolfran Suetter from Camp Worland and Fritz Hartung from Camp Dubois.[422]

A few former Wyoming prisoners of war returned to live in the United States after the war. Some former prisoners were sponsored by military personnel or farmers whose property they had worked on as prisoners. Former prisoners who returned to Wyoming to live include Ceasar Oriano from Camp Douglas and Fort Warren,[423] Julius Algermissen from Camp Douglas[424] and Robert Schultz from Camp Lovell.[425] Other former Wyoming prisoners returned to the United States and lived in other states. Otto Rechtnagle from Camp Douglas was sponsored by a U.S. sergeant he had met at the POW camp and moved to California to work for him. In addition, Otto Wietasch from the Ryan Park POW camp returned to the United States and settled in Pennsylvania.[426] Information shared by the former prisoners of war provides important firsthand accounts and insight into life in Wyoming POW camps.

POW ACKNOWLEDGEMENTS AND LABOR ACHIEVEMENTS

I n Wyoming, state and local agricultural agencies and timber industry contractors relied heavily on prisoner of war labor due to nationwide labor shortages. After some initial apprehension and concerns, local residents and civilian employers were very supportive and appreciative of the work conducted by the prisoners. The importance of the work done by POWs in tending and harvesting Wyoming's crops, and at the timber camps, was recognized by state and county agricultural and timber industry groups.[427]

State and local county and industry representatives and U.S. military officials from the POW base camps provided annual reports of labor achievements by the prisoners of war in Wyoming. In early December 1943, headlines in a Douglas newspaper announced, "Prisoner Labor Saved Crop Harvest in County This Year." The Converse County Agent reported that the county crop harvests could not have been successfully completed without the help of the Italian prisoners of war. He praised the cheerful and efficient manner in which the prisoners worked. The county agent specified the prisoners' achievements, which included the harvest of approximately 2,300 tons of beets, 86,000 bushels of potatoes, 310,000 pounds of beans and 2,000 tons of hay baled.[428] In order to provide some additional relevancy to the significance of the Camp Douglas POW accomplishments, it was calculated that the prisoners had harvested enough "sugar, in beets, to supply a city" of more than one million people "for one year, with all the sugar" permitted under the current rationing that was imposed.[429]

In 1944, military reports specified that the prisoners of war worked in Wyoming a total of 79,815 man-days in agriculture and "7,117 man-days in the timber industry." The Laramie County Agent credited the German POWs who worked in the Pine Bluffs area for "saving the potato and sugar beet crops." As the 1945 harvests were completed, prisoner of war accomplishments and statistics were reported across the state. According to Director A.E. Bowman of the Wyoming Agricultural Extension Service, in a letter he wrote to Governor Lester Hunt in September 1945, "it would have been impossible to satisfy the state's labor requirements for agriculture without the prisoners."[430]

10

CONCLUSION

The World War II POW camps of Wyoming were operated efficiently and successfully. The prisoners of war incarcerated in Wyoming POW camps were properly housed and well fed, in accordance with Geneva Convention guidelines, by the U.S. military personnel who operated the camps. In addition, the prisoners were treated well and respectfully. As awareness of potentially dangerous prisoners, conflicts and safety concerns within the camps were recognized by camp officials, changes in the methods used for evaluation and segregation of hostile prisoners and additional camp security measures were made to improve conditions in the camps. In correspondence with local residents after the war and in postwar interviews, former POWs acknowledged that they appreciated being treated and fed well while in Wyoming POW camps.

The prisoner of war labor helped to ensure that Wyoming agricultural crops and timber were successfully harvested. The prisoners were encouraged to be engaged in work projects to keep them occupied, and at the same time they provided critically needed labor for labor-intensive agricultural and timber work. Annual reports of the harvest of Wyoming crops provide specific details of the total harvest yields in 1943–45 using war prisoner labor. In addition, the prisoners were paid for their labor, which allowed them to purchase items they wanted while they were incarcerated at the POW camps and to save money for when they returned to their home countries.

Many positive relationships developed among camp military personnel, civilian employers and the prisoners. Local farmers and timber contractors were thankful for the prisoner of war labor. In turn, the fair treatment and kindness shown by the American POW camp staff and local residents were appreciated by the prisoners. Many Wyoming residents had Italian and German roots. Wyoming farmers fed the prisoners home-cooked meals or snacks to supplement their food rations. To show their appreciation, prisoners created artwork, wood carvings or other gifts for local residents. Several Wyoming residents and former POWs corresponded for many years after the war. In addition, several former POWs returned to Wyoming to visit or live. Some Wyoming residents also visited former POWs in their home countries. The U.S. military personnel, local residents and prisoners—despite their differences—worked together to cope with the challenges of the war and the everyday life of the prisoners in the World War II POW camps of Wyoming.

NOTES

Introduction

1. Krammer, *Nazi Prisoners of War in America*, 45, 77, 107, 113.
2. Thompson, *Men in German Uniform*, 1, 130.
3. Krammer, *Nazi Prisoners of War*, xiv, 28.
4. Larson, *Wyoming's War Years*, 220; Bangerter, "German Prisoners of War," 71, 82–91; "Powell's WWII German Prisoners of War," exhibit information, Homesteader Museum, Powell, Wyoming.
5. Thompson, *Men in German Uniform*, 2–3; Krammer, *Nazi Prisoners of War*, 41.
6. Krammer, *Nazi Prisoners of War*, 26, 28.
7. "Douglas POW Camp Will Close on Feb 1," *Douglas Enterprise*, January 22, 1946.
8. Taylor, *F.E. Warren Air Force Base*, 7, 85.
9. Krammer, *Nazi Prisoners of War*, 35.
10. "Powell's WWII German Prisoners of War"; "Four Labor Camps for Beet Help," *Goshen News*, September 20, 1945.
11. Larson, *Wyoming's War Years*, 220; "Powell's WWII German Prisoners of War."
12. Larson, *Wyoming's War Years*, 219–20; Bangerter, "German Prisoners of War," 83, 85; "German Prisoners Will Work in Timber Camps Southwest of Here," *Laramie Republican*, April 7, 1944.
13. Kip MacMillan, personal interview with author, September 29, 2014.

Chapter 1

14. Krammer, *Nazi Prisoners of War*, 26.

15. Taylor, *F.E. Warren Air Force Base*, 7; Bangerter, "German Prisoners of War," 73–91; National Guard Museum, Cheyenne, Wyoming, written communication, March 21, 2018; "Powell's WWII German Prisoners of War."

16. Larson, *Wyoming's War Years*, 206, 217, 220; "Powell's WWII German Prisoners of War."

17. Krammer, *Nazi Prisoners of War*, 82, 86–87, 107; "Italian Prisoner Camps Are Aiding in Labor Shortage," *Laramie Daily Bulletin*, September 29, 1943, box 21, folder 9, news clippings, UW War Activities Council, Collection #300002, American Heritage Center, University of Wyoming.

18. "Convention Relative to the Treatment of Prisoners of War, Geneva, July 27, 1929," International Committee of Red Cross, http://www.icrc.org/ihl/305; "Camp Douglas Officers' Club State Historic Site," Wyoming State Parks, Historic Sites and Trails; Harold Harlamert Camp Dubois records, 1944–1946, courtesy Linda Siemens.

19. Krammer, *Nazi Prisoners of War*, 79–80; Harlamert Camp Dubois Records.

20. Krammer, *Nazi Prisoners of War*, 80, 88.

21. Ibid., 50, 79–80, 83–84; Thompson, *Men in German Uniform*, 83–84; Larson, *Wyoming's War Years*, 218.

22. "Some Italian Prisoners to Be Placed on Honor," *Casper Tribune Herald*, October 30, 1943, American Heritage Center, University of Wyoming; Krammer, *Nazi Prisoners of War*, 283.

23. "Italian Prisoners Now Used for Army Work, McElroy Says," *Laramie Daily Bulletin*, April 25, 1944, American Heritage Center, University of Wyoming; Ellen Oriano Thompson, written communication with author, April 15, 2018.

24. Hansen, "Oral History Transcript," Wyoming State Archives; Walter Kurcon, August 23, 1988, correspondence, in *Wind Pudding and Rabbit Tracks: A History of Goshen County, Wyoming*, 293; Stutz, "Oral History Transcript WWII POW."

25. Thompson, *Men in German Uniform*, 43–44; Ellen Oriano Thompson, written communication with author, April 15, 2018; Hansen, "Oral History Transcript"; Stutz, "Oral History Transcript WWII POW."

26. Krammer, *Nazi Prisoners of War*, 49–50, 149; Thompson, *Men in German Uniform*, 38–39.

27. Krammer, *Nazi Prisoners of War*, 167, 174–80.

28. Leonard, *West of Yesteryear*, 197; Bangerter, "German Prisoners of War," 95.

29. Larson, *Wyoming's War Years*, 218–19; Paula Taylor, Warren ICBM and Heritage Museum, F.E. Warren Air Force Base, personal interviews with author and site visit, June 15, 2018.

30. Larson, *Wyoming's War Years*, 219–20; Kurcon, in *Wind Pudding and Rabbit Tracks*, 293.

31. U.S. War Department, "Prisoner of War Camp Labor Reports," Camp Dubois, Wyoming, 1944–1946, Office of Provost Marshal General, National Archives.

32. Krammer, *Nazi Prisoners of War*, 47, 83; "Two Escaped Prisoners Captured Same Day," *Torrington Telegram*, October 5, 1944; "Army Warns Against Wearing PW Marking," *Douglas Budget*, May 3, 1945.

33. Larson, *Wyoming's War Years*, 218–19; Bangerter, "German Prisoners of War," 74–76, 80.

34. Harlamert, Camp Dubois Records; Bangerter, "German Prisoners of War," 96.

35. Stutz, "Oral History Transcript WWII POW"; Robert Stottler, Washakie Museum & Cultural Center, "The Germans Are Coming" (undated); Ron Wilhelm, telephone interview with author, February 22, 2019; Harlamert, Camp Dubois Records.

36. Bangerter, "German Prisoners of War," 96, 98–99.

37. Krammer, *Nazi Prisoners of War*, 159; Stutz, "Oral History Transcript."

38. Stutz, "Oral History Transcript."

39. Krammer, *Nazi Prisoners of War*, 196, 209, 212.

40. Ibid., 202, 206, 208–9.

41. Bangerter, "German Prisoners of War," 75, 79; Leonard, *West of Yesteryear*, 199.

42. Krammer, *Nazi Prisoners of War*, 224–25.

43. Harlamert, Camp Dubois Records; U.S. War Department, "Prisoner of War Labor Reports."

44. Krammer, *Nazi Prisoners of War*, 4.

45. Ibid.

46. Ibid., 4–5.

47. Harlamert, Camp Dubois Records; Krammer, *Nazi Prisoners of War*, 4.

48. Johann Pilhofer, written and Skype interviews with author, April 6, 2017.

49. Krammer, *Nazi Prisoners of War*, 38–39.

50. Ibid., Johann Pilhofer, interviews with author; Stutz, "Oral History Transcript."

51. Krammer, *Nazi Prisoners of War*, 136, 139, 140, 145–46.

52. Larson, *Wyoming's War Years*, 220; Bangerter, "German Prisoners of War," 76–77, 81–82.

53. Larson, *Wyoming's War Years*, 220; "Two Escaped Prisoners of War Captured Same Day," *Torrington Telegram*, October 5, 1944; Bangerter, "German Prisoners of War," 90.

54. Krammer, *Nazi Prisoners of War*, 140–42.

55. Richard Lenz, Clearmont Community Oral History Tapes, courtesy Cynthia Vannoy; Leonard Brightly, written communication with author, September 4, 2018; Rich Fink, personal interview with author, March 16, 2018.

56. Taylor, *F.E. Warren Air Force Base*, 85.

57. Shayne Boutte, Fort Riley, Kansas National Cemetery, written communication with author, April 30, 2019.

58. Bangerter, "German Prisoners of War," 87.

59. Standard Death Certificate, Max Stoll, Wyoming Department of Health, August 28, 1945.

60. "Believe War Prisoner Lost Life in Canal," *Goshen County News*, August 16, 1945; Harold Harlamert, correspondence, November 13, 1945, courtesy Linda Siemens.

Chapter 2

61. "Douglas POW Camp Will Close on February 1," *Douglas Enterprise*, January 22, 1946.

62. "Camp Douglas Officers' Club State Historic Site," brochure, Wyoming State Parks, Historic Sites & Trails.

63. Ibid.; Larson, *Wyoming's War Years*, 217–18.

64. Larson, *Wyoming's War Years*, 218; U.S. War Department, Douglas Internment Camp, Douglas, Wyoming, General Layout, U.S. Engineer Office, Omaha, Nebraska, Camp Douglas Officers' Club State Historic Site.

65. Leonard, *West of Yesteryear*, "When Douglas Hosted Unusual Company," 196; Larson, *Wyoming's War Years*, 218; "Douglas POW Camp Will Close on February 1."

66. "Converse Labor, Inc., Formed to Secure Work of Prisoners." *Douglas Budget*, August 12, 1943.

67. "Prisoner Labor Contract Signed." *Douglas Budget*, August 26, 1943.

68. "Company of Military Police Arrive at the Prison Camp," *Douglas Budget*, August 12, 1943.

69. "First Group War Prisoners Arrived Here Last Friday," *Douglas Budget*, August 19, 1943; "412 Italian Prisoners Arrived Here Friday," *Douglas Enterprise*, August 17, 1943.

70. "War Prisoner Labor Now Being Used for Harvest," *Douglas Enterprise* September 23, 1943.

71. "1000 More Italian Prisoners Come Last Night; Two Trains," *Douglas Enterprise*, September 30, 1943; "Something About the Prisoners of War," *Douglas Budget*, December 9, 1943.

72. "Over a Thousand Italian War Prisoners Now Out on Various Work Projects," *Douglas Enterprise*, October 21, 1943; "Beet Harvest Nearly Completed," *Douglas Enterprise*, November 11, 1943.

73. "War Prisoners to Cut Down Timber," *Douglas Enterprise*, November 18, 1943; "War Prisoners to Be Trained in Timber Industry," *Douglas Enterprise*, November 30, 1943.

74. "German Prisoners Good Workmen," *Douglas Budget*, April 27, 1944.

75. Larson, *Wyoming's War Years*, 218; "Trainload of German Prisoners Arrive at POW Camp Tuesday," *Douglas Budget*, September 21, 1944.

76. "Trainload of German Prisoners Arrive at POW Camp Tuesday."

77. Leonard, *West of Yesteryear*, 197.

78. Bangerter, "German Prisoners of War," 79–80.

79. "POW Hiding at Camp," *Douglas Budget*, October 5, 1944; Bangerter, "German Prisoners of War," 80.

80. "Something About the Prisoners of War," *Douglas Budget*, December 9, 1943; Larson, *Wyoming's War Years*, 218–19.

81. "Camp Douglas Officers' Club State Historic Site."

82. Bangerter, "German Prisoners of War," 80; Leonard, *West of Yesteryear*, 198–99.

83. Ellen Oriano Thompson, written communication with author, April 15, 2018, May 1, 2019; Peg Layton Leonard, "POW Camp Was Douglas War Prize," undated, display board, Wyoming Pioneer Memorial Museum.

84. Leonard, *West of Yesteryear*, 200; Larson, *Wyoming's War Years*, 218.

85. Leonard, *West of Yesteryear*, 200.

86. Larson, *Wyoming's War Years*, 220.

87. Bangerter, "German Prisoners of War," 81–82.

88. Shayne Boutte, Fort Riley, Kansas National Cemetery, written communication, April 30, 2019; Dr. Robert Smith, curator, Fort Riley,

Kansas Museum, telephone and written communication, April 24, 2019; Leonard, *West of Yesteryear*, 198.

89. "Italian Captain Buried," *Douglas Budget*, March 16, 1944.

90. Leonard, *West of Yesteryear*, 198.

91. "Only a Few Prisoners Left at the Camp," *Douglas Budget*, January 24, 1946.

92. "Camp to Be Deactivated Early in Feb," *Douglas Budget*, January 24, 1946.

93. Leonard, *West of Yesteryear*, 196.

94. "To Move Camp Buildings," *Douglas Budget*, July 4, 1946; "POW Camp Materials Now Being Sold," *Douglas Budget*, November 28, 1946.

95. "Prisoner Camp Hospital Now County Property," *Douglas Budget*, September 12, 1946.

96. "Workers Dismantle Douglas POW Camp in Record Time," *Douglas Budget*, November 20, 1946.

97. Richard Fink, personal interview and written correspondence with author, April 8, 2018.

98. Leonard, *West of Yesteryear*, 197; "Camp Douglas Officer's Club State Historic Site."

99. Taylor, personal interviews with author, June 6, 2018, and June 15, 2018.

100. Taylor, *F.E. Warren Air Force Base*, 7, 85.

101. Bangerter, "German Prisoners of War," 73.

102. Taylor, personal interviews with author and site visits, June 2018; Bangerter, "German Prisoners of War," 74.

103. Larson, *Wyoming's War Years*, 206; Taylor, personal interviews with author and site visits, June 2018.

104. Thompson, written and personal communication with the author, April 15, 2018, August 13, 2018; Larson, *Wyoming's War Years*, 206.

105. Thompson, written communication with author, April 15, 2018.

106. Fort D.A. Russel, Wyoming Post Plans, Warren ICBM and Heritage Museum; Bangerter, "German Prisoners of War," 74.

107. Fort D.A. Russel Post Plans; Taylor, personal interviews with author, June 2018; Fort Warren POW Camp site visit by author, June 15, 2018.

108. Thompson, written communication with the author, April 15, 2018, February 3, 2019; Bangerter, "German Prisoners of War, 76.

109. Bangerter, "German Prisoners of War," 75.

110. Ibid., 75–76.

111. Krammer, *Nazi Prisoners of War*, 132; "Escaped Nazi War Prisoners Caught West of Cheyenne," *Rock Springs Miner*, June 11, 1944, box 21, folder 9, news clippings, UW War Activities Council, Collection #300002; Bangerter, "German Prisoners of War," 76–77.

112. Taylor, *F.E. Warren Air Force Base*, 85.

113. Taylor, personal interviews with author and site visits, June 2018; "PWs Buried in Wyoming," http://www.gentracer.org/powdeathindex.html.

114. "Francis E. Warren Air Force Base Cemetery Grave Guide" (revised 1996), 9–10.

115. Warren ICBM and Heritage Museum, exhibit information, F.E. Warren Air Force Base, Cheyenne.

Chapter 3

116. "Harvest Will Employ Nearly 100 Prisoners of War," *Pine Bluffs Post*, September 9, 1943; "Four Labor Camps For Beet Help," *Goshen County News*, September 20, 1945; U.S. War Department, "Prisoner of War Labor Reports," Camp Dubois, Wyoming, 1944–1946, Office of the Provost Marshal General, National Archives.

117. "Last of Nazi Prisoners Leaving Camp Today, Small Staff Remains," *Scottsbluff Star-Herald*, March 15, 1946; Camp Scottsbluff plans, Legacy of the Plains Museum, Gering, Nebraska.

118. Amanda Gibbs, Legacy of the Plains Museum, Gering, Nebraska, written communication with author, January 3–7, 2019.

119. Marsh, *Nebraska POW Camps*, 52, 54.

120. "Italian Prisoner Camps Are Aiding in Labor Shortage," *Laramie Daily Bulletin*, September 29, 1943.

121. Marsh, *Nebraska POW Camps*, 65–69.

122. Ibid., 57–59.

123. Ibid., 57.

124. Bangerter, "German Prisoners of War," 95.

125. Krammer, *Nazi Prisoners of War*, 169–70.

126. Ibid., 134.

127. "Last of Nazi Prisoners Leaving Camp Today; Small Staff Remains" *Scottsbluff Star-Herald*, March 15, 1946, Legacy of the Plains Museum.

128. Marsh, *Nebraska POW Camps*, 53, 71; Dennis Wecker, personal interview with author, April 19, 2018; Scottsbluff POW camp site visit by author, September 25, 2018.

Chapter 4

129. During my research on Big Horn County POW camps, from 2016 to 2018, many oral interviews of local residents were conducted by the author and Karen Spragg, president, Lovell-Kane Area Museum. The interviews have been transcribed and shared with area residents during public presentations and in local newspaper articles. The information obtained from the oral interviews includes a wide range of historical details and memories relating to Big Horn County POW camps. Although not all the content of the interviews is included in this book, the information obtained has been added to both the Wyoming World War II POW camps research project records and the local museum records.

130. "Agency Asks for War Prisoners to Work," *Basin Republican Rustler*, April 27, 1944.

131. "Farm Labor Situation for Coming Season Is Explained," *Basin Republican Rustler*, April 13, 1944.

132. "Agency Asks for War Prisoners to Work."

133. "Large Beet Harvest Begins This Week," *Basin Republican Rustler*, September 28, 1944.

134. "Guards and Prisoners Left Basin Thursday," *Basin Republican Rustler*, November 9, 1944.

135. "First Sugar Beet Labor Arrives," *Basin Republican Rustler*, May 31, 1945.

136. "War Prisoners Are Available for Labor," *Basin Republican Rustler*, June 7, 1945.

137. "War Prisoners Finish Thinning Sugar Beets" *Basin Republican Rustler*, July 26, 1945.

138. "Beet Harvest Starts Tuesday Sept. 25," *Basin Republican Rustler*, September 13, 1945.

139. "Rain Slows Work," *Basin Republican Rustler*, September 20, 1945.

140. "Sugar Beet Crop About 55% Harvested," *Basin Republican Rustler*, October 18, 1945.

141. "War Prisoners Finish Thinning Sugar Beets," *Basin Republican Rustler*, July 26, 1945.

142. Bangerter, "German Prisoners of War," 106–7.

143. Ibid.

144. Ibid., 110–11.

145. Barbara Greene, telephone interview with author, August 13, 2018.

146. Tom Black, telephone interview with author, August 14, 2018.

147. Robert Gish, personal interview with author, March 16, 2018.

148. "CCC Camp Becomes Basin's Property," *Basin Republican Rustler*, May 6, 1946.

149. Basin POW camp site visit by author, August 10, 2018; Sheila Paumer, Big Horn County Fair operations manager, telephone interview with author, February 26, 2019.

150. "War Prisoners to Be Available Here Soon," *Lovell Chronicle*, May 31, 1945; *State of Wyoming Biennial Report of the Wyoming National Guard for the Years 1923 and 1924, 1925 and 1926*, Wyoming National Guard Museum, Cheyenne, Wyoming; Allen Sessions, telephone interview with author, July 2, 2018.

151. "War Prisoners to Be Available Here Soon."

152. "Many Beet Workers Arrive in This Area," *Lovell Chronicle*, June 7, 1945.

153. "War Prisoners Finish Thinning Sugar Beets," *Deaver Sentinel and Frannie Independent*, July 27, 1945.

154. "Beet Digging to Start on Tuesday," *Lovell Chronicle*, September 20, 1945; "Sugar Beet Harvest Completed This Week," *Deaver Sentinel and Frannie Independent*, November 2, 1945.

155. Thales Haskell, personal interview with Karen Spragg, president, Lovell-Kane Area Museum, May 2, 2018.

156. Peggy Luthy, telephone interview with author, June 25, 2018.

157. Rich Fink, personal interview with author, March 16, 2018.

158. Thomas Tippetts, email correspondence, February 24, 2018.

159. Gary Goodrich, telephone interview with author and written correspondence, August 29, 2018.

160. Tim Townsend, telephone interview with author, September 6, 2018.

161. Robert H. Schultz obituary information, Karen Spragg, president, Lovell-Kane Area Museum, June 20, 2018.

162. "War Prisoners to Be Available Here Soon"; "Sugar Beet Harvest Completed This Week," *Deaver Sentinel and Frannie Independent*, November 2, 1945.

163. Gimmeson, *German POW Camp in Deaver*, 23.

164. Leonard Brightly, telephone interview and written correspondence with author, September 4, 2018; Camp Deaver photograph, CCC Camp BR-7, Camp Photograph 1935, RG 115 Entry 21 Box 7, Regional National Archives, Broomfield, Colorado, courtesy Robert Audretsch.

165. Gimmeson, *German POW Camp in Deaver*, 23.

166. Paul Lewis, telephone interview with author, March 23, 2018.

167. Gimmeson, *German POW Camp in Deaver*, 19.

168. Ibid., 35; Bangerter, "German Prisoners of War," 84.

169. "War Prisoners to Be Available Here Soon"; "Beet Harvest Starts Tuesday Sept. 25," *Basin Republican Rustler*, September 13, 1945.
170. "Sugar Beet Harvest Completed This Week," *Deaver Sentinel and the Frannie Independent*, November 2, 1945.
171. Gimmeson, *German POW Camp in Deaver*, 44.
172. Ibid., 43–44; Johanna K. Gimmeson, personal interview with author, August 16, 2018.
173. Fred and Florence Wambeke, personal interviews with author, August 15, 2016, and March 16, 2018.
174. Paul Lewis, telephone interview with author, March 23, 2018.
175. Stanley Partridge, telephone interview with author, March 23, 2018.
176. Buck Homewood, personal interview with author, March 16, 2018.
177. Ernst Ruehling painting and label, author museum visit and review, August 16, 2018, courtesy the Homesteader Museum.
178. Leonard Brightly, telephone interview and written correspondence with author, September 4, 2018.
179. Ibid.
180. Dennis Godfrey, telephone interview and written communication with author, August 29, 2018.
181. Leonard Brightly, telephone interview and written correspondence with author, September 4, 2018.
182. Ibid.
183. Ibid.
184. Gimmeson, *German POW Camp in Deaver*, 45; Fred Wambeke, personal interviews and former POW camp site visit with author, August 15, 2016.
185. "Powell's WWII German Prisoners of War," Homesteader Museum; Gimmeson, *German POW Camp in Deaver*, 20.
186. "Nazi War Prisoners Are Housed at Powell," *Northern Wyoming Daily News*, October 18, 1945.
187. Gimmeson, *German POW Camp in Deaver*, 42.
188. "German Prisoners Help Framers of Valley with Fall Crop," *Powell Tribune*, September 28, 1944, courtesy Ron Blevins.
189. Ruby Hopkins, telephone interview with author, November 8, 2018.
190. "Italian Workers Arrive to Help in Beet Harvest," *Northern Wyoming Daily News*, October 1, 1943.
191. "War Prisoners Scheduled to Arrive Tomorrow" *Northern Wyoming Daily News*, September 29, 1943.
192. Harold Harlamert, photo captions, P.W. Branch Camp, Worland, Wyoming, July 1944, courtesy Linda Siemens.

193. "Italian Workers Arrive to Help in Beet Harvest."

194. "Sugar Beet Campaign Underway," *Northern Wyoming Daily News*, October 2, 1943.

195. "Sugar Harvest Ends Today," *Northern Wyoming Daily News*, November 4, 1943.

196. "War Prisoners Arrive to Work in Beet Fields," *Northern Wyoming Daily News*, June 10, 1944.

197. "Germans Refuse to Thin Beets in Local Fields," *Northern Wyoming Daily News*, June 21, 1944; "Action Taken to Get Prisoners to Return to Work," *Casper Tribune Herald*, June 22, 1944, American Heritage Center, University of Wyoming.

198. Krammer, *Nazi Prisoners of War*, 112.

199. "Nazi War Prisoners Appeal to Adolf," *Northern Wyoming Daily News*, June 22, 1944; "Action Taken to Get Prisoners to Return to Work."

200. "Nazi POWs Agree to Go Back to Work," *Northern Wyoming Daily News*, June 24, 1944.

201. "Prisoner of War Camp to Close Tomorrow," *Northern Wyoming Daily News*, July 15, 1944.

202. Bangerter, "German Prisoners of War," 91.

203. Ibid.

204. Bob Gross, "Former POW Returns to Worland," *Northern Wyoming Daily News*, May 16, 1983.

205. "Beet Harvest Underway in Worland District," *Northern Wyoming Daily News*, September 29, 1945.

206. "Storm Brings Harvest to End," *Northern Wyoming Daily News*, November 9, 1945.

207. "Prisoners and Mexican Nationals Did Bulk of Harvest Reports Show," *Northern Wyoming Daily News*, November 22, 1945.

208. Gerry Geis, telephone interview with author, June 18, 2018.

209. Lloyd Lungren, telephone interview with author, June 19, 2018.

210. Pendergraft, *Washakie*, 189.

211. Clint Corneal, telephone interview with author, September 12, 2018.

212. Bob Gross, "Former POW Returns to Worland," *Northern Wyoming Daily News*, May 16, 1983.

213. Ibid.

214. Lloyd Lungren, telephone interview with author, July 2, 2018.

215. Cynthia Vannoy, "Clearmont Camp Marks 50 Years," *Sheridan Press*, July 7, 1995; Dick Lenz, "Prisoner of War Camp at Clearmont," March 1982; "War Prisoners to Be Available Soon"; Bangerter, "German Prisoners of War," 83.

216. Alik Kaufman, Clearmont Community History Oral History Tapes, courtesy Cynthia Vannoy; Pauline Schuman, *Backward Glance 1880s–1980s, Ulm, Leiter, Ucross, Clearmont, a Century of History* (Clearmont, WY: Clearmont Historical Group, 1993), 593.

217. Rose Fowler, Clearmont Community History Oral History Tapes, courtesy Cynthia Vannoy.

218. Alex Pitsch, Clearmont Community History Oral History Tapes, courtesy Cynthia Vannoy.

219. Richard Lenz, Clearmont Community History Oral History Tapes, courtesy Cynthia Vannoy; Russel Huson, *Backward Glance 1880s–1980s*, 460.

220. Zach Garretson, telephone interview with author, August 7, 2018.

221. Claud Bolinger, *Backward Glance 1880s–1980s*, 680.

222. Erin Quarterman, *Backward Glance 1880s–1980s*, 357–58; Alik Kaufman, Clearmont Community History Oral History Tapes, courtesy Cynthia Vannoy.

223. Rose Fowler, Clearmont Community History Oral History Tapes, courtesy Cynthia Vannoy.

224. Rose Fowler, Alex Pitsch, Clearmont Community History Oral History Tapes, courtesy Cynthia Vannoy.

225. Rose Fowler, Clearmont Oral History Tapes, 9–10, courtesy Cynthia Vannoy.

226. Kelly Weber, *Backward Glance 1880s–1980s*, 644.

227. Steve Switzer, personal interview with author, May 17, 2018.

228. Ann Roebling, personal interview and POW camp site visit with author, May 17, 2018.

Chapter 5

229. "Labor Board Seeks to Keep Prisoners Throughout the Summer," *Riverton Review*, June 28, 1945; "Imported Labor Being Returned," *Riverton Review*, November 8, 1945.

230. Fritz Rein, telephone and personal interviews with author, January 25, 2018, February 2, 2018; Tony Swasso, personal interviews with author, January 10, 2018, January 18, 2018.

231. "Officers Inspect Local Site for Prisoner Camp," *Riverton Review*, March 8, 1945; *State of Wyoming Biennial Report of the Wyoming National Guard for the Years 1925 and 1926*, Wyoming National Guard Museum, Cheyenne, Wyoming.

232. "Work Is Started on POW Accommodations." *Riverton Review*, April 12, 1945.

233. Swasso, personal interviews with author, January 10, 2018, January 18, 2018.

234. "Labor Board Seeks to Keep Prisoners Throughout Summer." *Riverton Review*, June 28, 1945.

235. Barbara Cipolla, personal interview with author, May 17, 2018.

236. "German POWs Begin Working Today in Local Beet Fields," *Riverton Review*, September 27, 1945.

237. "Harvest Labor Shortage Becomes Acute Problem," *Riverton Review*, September 20, 1945.

238. Bob Sauer, personal interviews with author, January 10, 2018, January 18, 2018.

239. Paul Sauer, personal interviews with author, January 10, 2018, January 18, 2018.

240. Rein, telephone and personal interviews with author, January 25, 2018, February 2, 2018.

241. Gayle Currah, telephone interview with author, January 8, 2018.

242. Allison, *Dubois*, *Wyoming Area History*, 2–3; Pinkerton, *Knights of the Broadax*, 169–71.

243. Harold Harlamert, "He'll Not Forget a Christmas Near Dubois," *Riverton Ranger*, December 22, 1983.

244. Harlamert, correspondence, December 12, 1944.

245. Ibid., September 7, 1945.

246. Ibid., January 15, 1945.

247. Harlamert, Camp Dubois Records.

248. Harlamert, correspondence, October 22, 1945.

249. Ibid., November 5, 1945.

250. Ibid., August 27, 1945.

251. Ibid., July 17, 1945.

252. Ibid., December 25, 1944.

253. Harlamert, "He'll Not Forget a Christmas."

254. Harlamert, correspondence, November 5, 1945.

255. Ibid.

256. Fritz Hartung, "German Ex-Soldier Visits POW Camp," *Wyoming Journal*, August 28, 1975.

257. Harlamert, correspondence, July 31, 1945.

258. U.S. War Department, P.O.W. Branch Camp, Dubois, Wyoming, Site Plan, June 27, 1945; P.O.W. Kitchen and Mess Hall, June 29, 1945; E.M. Kitchen and Mess Hall, June 30, 1945; site plan showing Washrooms, Latrines, Tool Shed and Root Cellar, July 2, 1945, Office of Post Engineer, Scottsbluff, Nebraska.

259. Harlamert, "He'll Not Forget a Christmas."

260. Johann Pilhofer, written and Skype interview with author, April 6, 2017.

261. U.S. War Department, P.O.W. Branch Camp, Dubois, Wyoming, Site Plan.

262. Harlamert, "He'll Not Forget a Christmas."

263. U.S. War Department, P.O.W. Branch Camp, Dubois, Wyoming, Site Plan.

264. Ibid.

265. Harlamert, correspondence, July 17, 1945.

266. Ibid., October 9, 1945.

267. U.S. War Department, P.O.W. Branch Camp, Dubois, Wyoming, Site Plan.

268. Harlamert, correspondence, October 9, 1945.

269. Harlamert, Camp Dubois Photo Captions, 1944–45.

270. Katrine Vandermeulen, personal communication with author, January 25, 2015.

271. Harlamert, correspondence, November 13, 1945.

272. Harlamert, correspondence January 15, 1945.

273. U.S. War Department, "Prisoner of War Camp Labor Reports."

274. Ibid., December 12, 1944.

275. Ibid., December 26, 1944.

276. Joseph Zwijacz, written interview and correspondence with author, April 21, 2016.

277. Edna Hartung, personal communication with author, January 26, 2015.

278. Harlamert, Camp Dubois Records.

279. Bangerter, "German Prisoners of War," 91–121.

280. Ibid., 99–100.

281. Ibid., 95–96.

282. Ibid., 96, 99.

283. Carl Hartung, personal communication with author, January 29, 2015.

284. Fritz Hartung, "German Ex-Soldier Visits POW Camp," *Wyoming Journal*, August 28, 1975.

285. Harlamert, correspondence, July 17, 1945.

286. Ibid., September 7, 1945.

287. Harlamert, correspondence, July 31, 1945; Frederick Niedner Jr., email and telephone communication with author, June 14–20, 2019.

288. Johann Pilhofer, written and Skype interview with author, April 6, 2017.

289. Ibid.

290. Ibid.

291. Ibid.

292. Ibid.

293. Ibid.

294. Harlamert, correspondence, December 12, 1944.

295. Ibid., August 21, 1945.

296. Ibid., December 25, 1944.

297. Local resident interviews with author, 2014–16.

298. Kip MacMillan, interview with author, September 29, 2014.

299. "Local Citizenry against Beer for German Prisoners," *Riverton Review*, August 10, 1944.

300. Camp Dubois site visits by author, July–September 2015.

301. Ibid.

Chapter 6

302. Melody Newell, personal interview and POW camp site visit with author, October 21, 2017.

303. Bangerter, "German Prisoners of War," 85.

304. "Few Prisoners Left for Labor," *Douglas Budget*, June 22, 1944.

305. Bangerter, "German Prisoners of War," 85.

306. Peg Layton Leonard, *West of Yesteryear*, 200.

307. Newell, POW camp site visit with author, October 21, 2017.

308. "Centennial CCC Camp Will House Nazi PW Labor," *Saratoga Sun*, July 26, 1945, box 21, folder 9, news clippings, UW War Activities Council, Collection #300002.

309. Jerry Hansen, personal interview and POW camp site visit with author, July 21, 2018.

310. "Centennial CCC Camp Will House Nazi PW Labor."

311. Bangerter, "German Prisoners of War," 83.

312. Meryle Hansen Oral History Transcript, August 9, 1986, H2005-68, Ryan Park POW Camp Collection, Wyoming State Archives.

313. "War Prisoners Help to Relieve Labor Shortage in Timber Camps," *Saratoga Sun*, October 28, 1943.

314. Ibid.

315. Larson, *Wyoming's War Years*, 219.

316. "Fifty More Prisoners of War Brought Here for Work in Timber," *Saratoga Sun*, November 18, 1943.

317. Meryle Hansen Oral History Transcript, Wyoming State Archives.

318. Meryle Hansen Sketch of Ryan Park POW Camp, H2005-68, Ryan Park POW Camp Collection, Wyoming State Archives.

319. Candy Moulton, "German POWs Harvested Timber at Ryan Park during World War II," *Rawlins Daily Times*, compiled by Dick Perue of "Historical Reproductions by Perue," September 2016, from material in the Bob Martin/Dick Perue collection, *Saratoga Sun* and other sources.

320. Meryle Hansen Oral History Transcript, Wyoming State Archives.

321. "Camp at Ryan Park Now Being Prepared for German Prisoners, *Saratoga Sun*, May 18, 1944.

322. "War Prisoners Recently Employed Here Are Taken Back to Douglas," *Saratoga Sun*, April 13, 1944.

323. Meryle Hansen Oral History Transcript, Wyoming State Archives.

324. Larson, *Wyoming's War Years*, 220.

325. Meryle Hansen Oral History Transcript.

326. Ibid.

327. Ibid.

328. "Job Break-Down Sheet for Training Men on New Job," H2005-68, Ryan Park POW Camp Collection, Wyoming State Archives.

329. Meryle Hansen Oral History Transcript.

330. Ibid.

331. Art Bergquist, German Soldiers at Ryan Park, Photo Caption, H2005-68, Ryan Park POW Camp Collection, Wyoming State Archives.

332. Neal Ward, "Eating of Horse Flesh by POWS Tops Recollection of Events at Ryan Park Camp," 1992, Ryan Park World War II POW Camp information compiled by Dick Perue.

333. Larson, *Wyoming's War Years*, 220.

334. Meryle Hansen Oral History Transcript.

335. Dick Perue, written communication with author, February 2, 2019, February 19, 2019, Bob Martin/Dick Perue Collection, Historical Reproductions by Perue.

336. "Former War Prisoner Returns to Camp," *Saratoga Sun*, undated, H2005-68, Ryan Park POW Camp Collection, Wyoming State Archives.

337. Ryan Park POW camp site visit by author, July 20, 2018.

Chapter 7

338. "Over 1000 Prisoners from Douglas Camp Working Harvest," *Wheatland Times*, October 14, 1943, box 21, folder 9, news clippings, UW War Activities Council, Collection #300002.

339. "Prisoners of War Will Arrive Next Week for Beet Field Labor," *Wheatland Times*, May 4, 1944, box 21, folder 9, news clippings, UW War Activities Council, Collection #300002.

340. Harlamert, Photo Captions, Camp Wheatland POW Camp, undated, courtesy Linda Siemens.

341. "Prisoners of War Will Arrive Next Week for Beet Field Labor," *Wheatland Times*, May 4, 1944, box 21, folder 9, news clippings, UW War Activities Council, Collection #300002.

342. Bangerter, "German Prisoners of War," 89–90.

343. Ibid.

344. Ibid.

345. Denzil Cochran, written correspondence to Judy Wilson, Laramie Peak Museum, October 2018.

346. Ron Wilhelm, telephone interview with author, February 22, 2019.

347. Ibid.

348. Ibid.

349. Ibid.

350. Judy Wilson, Laramie Peak Museum, personal interview and POW camp site visit with author, October 16, 2017; Amy Huffer, Platte County Fairgrounds, telephone interview with author, February 22, 2019.

351. "Four Labor Camps for Beet Help," *Goshen County News*, September 20, 1945.

352. Ibid.

353. "Allocate More Prisoners of War to Goshen County the Past Week," *Torrington Telegram*, October 26, 1944.

354. "Labor Needs for County Are Figured," *Goshen County News*, February 22, 1945.

355. Larson, *Wyoming's War Years*, 220.

356. "Prisoner of War Labor Plan Asked," *Goshen County News*, January 25, 1945.

357. "Legion Post Is Opposed War Prisoner Paroling," *Goshen County News*, February 15, 1945.

358. Bangerter, "German Prisoners of War," 87.

359. David Eddington, personal interview and former POW camp site visit with author, June 7, 2018.

360. "More Labor Is Arriving Here Next Few Days," *Goshen County News*, June 7, 1945.

361. Beverly Jones Babcock, telephone interview with author, September 25, 2018; Beverly Jones, "Charley and Esther Jones Potato Warehouse," in *Wind Pudding and Rabbit Tracks: A History of Goshen County, Wyoming*, 320–21.

362. "Two Escaped Prisoners of War Captured Same Day," *Torrington Telegram*, October 5, 1944.

363. Shirley Heckart, personal interview with author, September 8, 2019.

364. Stutz, "Oral History Transcript WW II POW."

365. "More Labor Is Arriving Here Next Few Days," *Goshen County News*, June 7, 1945; "Four Labor Camps for Beet Help."

366. "Prisoners of War to Work on Farms, Ranches in Wyoming," *Laramie Republican Boomerang*, August 27, 1943; Walter Kurcon, August 23, 1988 correspondence, *Wind Pudding and Rabbit Tracks: A History of Goshen County*, 293.

367. "War Prisoners Labor," *Wheatland Times*, October 7, 1943.

368. "War Prisoners Labor"; Bangerter, "German Prisoners of War," 87.

369. "Prisoner of War Labor Now Located," *Torrington Telegram*, April 27, 1944.

370. "Prisoner of War Camp at Veteran," *Wind Pudding and Rabbit Tracks, A History of Goshen County*, 291–92.

371. Walter Kurcon, August 23, 1988, correspondence, *Wind Pudding and Rabbit Tracks*, 293.

372. Harold Hong, "YMCA Report on Visit to Prisoner of War Branch Camp (Scottsbluff), Veteran, WY," December 18, 1944, 1–3, National Archives.

373. Bangerter, "German Prisoners of War," 96.

374. Stutz, "Oral History Transcript WWII POW."

375. Ibid.

376. Ibid.

377. Ibid.

378. Ibid.

379. Ibid.

380. David Eddington, former CCC/POW Camp buildings identified on Camp Veteran photo, February 10, 2019; David Eddington, personal interview and POW camp site visit with author, June 7, 2018.

381. "More Labor Is Arriving Here Next Few Days"; "POWs Going Home," *Lingle Guide Review*, November 29, 1945.

382. Bangerter, "German Prisoners of War," 85; Harry Heller, telephone interviews with author, August 26, 2017 and October 11, 2017.

383. "Prisoner of War Camp for Lingle," *Goshen County News*, March 15, 1945.

384. "More Labor Is Arriving Here Next Few Days."

385. Harry Heller, telephone interviews with author, August 26, 2017 and October 11, 2017; Deanna Greenwald, telephone interview with author, September 24, 2018.

386. Mike Anderson, personal interviews and site visit with the author, June 6, 2018 and June 7, 2018.

387. Nancy (Hill) Zimmer, telephone interview with author, September 24, 2018; Adam and Eleanor Hill, *Wind Pudding and Rabbit Tracks*, vol. 2, 301–2; Robin Lippincott, *Wind Pudding and Rabbit Tracks*, 295–96.

388. Mary Quinonez, personal interview with author, September 23, 2018; Lippincott, *Wind Pudding and Rabbit Tracks*, 295.

389. Adam and Eleanor Hill, *Wind Pudding and Rabbit Tracks*, vol. 2, 301–2; Lippincott, *Wind Pudding and Rabbit Tracks*, 295–96.

390. Ruthanne (Hill) Hansen, telephone interview with author, September 25, 2018.

391. Mary Quinonez, personal interview with author, September 23, 2018.

392. Harry Heller, telephone interviews with author, August 26, 2017 and October 11, 2017.

393. "POWs Going Home," *Lingle Guide Review*, November 29, 1945.

394. "Four Labor Camps for Beet Help," *Goshen County News*, September 20, 1945; Lippincott, *Wind Pudding and Rabbit Tracks*, 293–96.

395. Larry Lippincott and Robin Schainost, personal interview and POW camp site visit with author, September 23, 2018; Lippincott, *Wind Pudding and Rabbit Tracks*, 293–96.

396. Larry Lippincott, personal interview and Camp Huntley site visit with author, September 23, 2018.

397. Ibid.

398. "Harvest Here Will Employ Nearly 100 Prisoners of War," *Pine Bluffs Post*, September 9, 1943; "War Prisoner Labor," *Wheatland Times*, October 7, 1943.

399. "Beet Crop Here This Year Less Than Half 1942," *Pine Bluffs Post*, November 4, 1943.

400. "Prisoner and Mexican Labor to Arrive Here Saturday," *Pine Bluffs Post*, September 21, 1944.

401. "Harvesting of Big Beet Crop Will Be Finished Tomorrow," *Pine Bluffs Post*, November 2, 1944.

402. "Many Large Yields Reported by Spud Growers This Year," *Pine Bluffs Post*, September 27, 1945.

403. "Farmers Wanting POW Help Should Make Application," *Pine Bluffs Post*, October 4, 1945.

404. Jean Bastian, ed., *History of Laramie County, Wyoming* (Dallas, TX: Curtis Media Corporation, 1987), 363, Pine Bluffs Branch Library.

405. Jack Harrison, telephone interview with author, June 12, 2018.

406. Don Strube, personal interview with author, May 31, 2018.

407. Ibid.

408. Norman Sanders, personal interview with author, June 14, 2018.

409. Richard Gardiner, telephone interview with author, June 14, 2018.

410. Norman Sanders, personal interview with author, June 14, 2018.

Chapter 8

411. Krammer, *Nazi Prisoners of War*, 226–27, 240; Harlamert, correspondence, September 10, 1945.

412. Harlamert, Camp Dubois Records; Kurcon, in *Wind Pudding and Rabbit Tracks*, 293.

413. "Camp to be Deactivated Early in February," *Douglas Budget*, January 24, 1946.

414. "Last of Nazi Prisoners Leaving Camp Today; Small Staff Remains," *Scottsbluff Star-Herald*, March 15, 1946, Legacy of the Plains Museum.

415. Taylor, *F.E. Warren Air Force Base*, 7.

416. Krammer, *Nazi Prisoners of War*, 237.

417. "Last of Nazi Prisoners Leaving Camp Today; Small Staff Remains"; "Camp to Be Deactivated Early in February."

418. Krammer, *Nazi Prisoners of War*, 255.

419. Ibid., 239, 247; Johann Pilhofer, Skype interview with author, April 6, 2017.

420. Stutz, "Oral History Transcript WWII POW."

421. Thompson, written communication with author, February 3, 2019; Larry Sprague, "Gerhard Arlt, From Germany to Colorado, Wyoming and Back," undated, unpublished.

422. Bob Gross, "Former POW Returns to Worland," *Northern Wyoming Daily News*, May 16, 1983; "German Ex-Soldier Visits POW Camp," *Wyoming Journal*, August 28, 1975.

423. Thompson, written communication with author, April 15, 2018.

424. Bangerter, "German Prisoners of War," 73; Leonard, *West of Yesteryear*, 201.

425. Robert H. Schultz obituary information, courtesy Karen Spragg, President, Lovell-Kane Area Museum, June 20, 2018.

426. Leonard, *West of Yesteryear*, 200–1. "Former War Prisoner Returns to Camp," *Saratoga Sun*, undated, H2005-68, Ryan Park POW Camp Collection, Wyoming State Archives.

Chapter 9

427. "Prisoner Labor Saved Crop Harvest in County This Year," *Douglas Enterprise*, December 7, 1943, box 21, folder 9, news clippings, UW War Activities Council, Collection #300002.

428. Ibid.

429. "Douglas War Prisoners Win Praise," *Wyoming State Tribune*, January 19, 1944, American Heritage Center, University of Wyoming.

430. Larson, *Wyoming's War Years*, 220.

BIBLIOGRAPHY

Allison, Mary. *Dubois, Wyoming Area History*. Dallas, TX: Curtis Media Corporation, 1991.

American Heritage Center. University of Wyoming. Box 21. Folder 9. Wyoming POW camps news clippings. UW War Activities Council. Collection #300002.

Backward Glance 1880s–1980s, Ulm, Leiter, Ucross, Clearmont: A Century of History. Clearmont, WY: Clearmont Historical Group, 1993.

Bangerter, Lowell A. "German Prisoners of War in Wyoming." *Journal of German-American Studies* 14, no. 2 (1979): 65–121.

Bastian, Jean, ed. *History of Laramie County, Wyoming*. Dallas, TX: Curtis Media Corporation, 1987. Pine Bluffs Branch Library.

"Convention Relative to the Treatment of Prisoners of War, Geneva, July 27, 1929." International Committee of the Red Cross, http://www.icrc.org/ihl/305.

Gimmeson, Johanna K. *German POW Camp in Deaver, Wyoming, 1944–1945*. 2014.

Hansen, Meryle. "Oral History Transcript." August 9, 1986. H2005-68. Ryan Park POW Camp Collection. Wyoming State Archives.

———. Sketch of Ryan Park POW Camp. H2005-68. Ryan Park POW Camp Collection. Wyoming State Archives.

"Job Break-Down Sheet for Training Men on New Job." H2005-68. Ryan Park POW Camp Collection. Wyoming State Archives.

Krammer, Arnold. *Nazi Prisoners of War in America*. Briarcliff Manor, New York: Stein and Day, 1979.

Larson, T.A. *Wyoming's War Years* 1941–1945. Laramie: University of Wyoming, 1954.

Leonard, Peg Layton. *West of Yesteryear.* "When Douglas Hosted Unusual Company." Boulder, CO: Johnson Publishing Company, 1976.

Marsh, Melissa Amateis. *Nebraska POW Camps: A History of World War II Prisoners in the Heartland.* Charleston, SC: The History Press, 2014.

National Guard of the United States. *1940 National Guard of the United States State of Wyoming.* Wyoming National Guard Museum, Cheyenne, Wyoming.

Pendergraft, Ray. *Washakie: A Wyoming History.* Austin, TX: Saddlebag Books. 1985.

Pinkerton, Joan Trego, *Knights of the Broadax.* Caldwell, ID: Caxton Printers, Ltd., 1981.

Standard Death Certificate. Max Stoll. Wyoming Department of Health. August 28, 1945.

State of Wyoming Biennial Report of the Wyoming National Guard for the Years 1923 and 1924, 1925 and 1926. Wyoming National Guard Museum, Cheyenne, Wyoming.

Stutz, Paul. "Oral History Transcript WWII POW." Wyoming State Museum. May 20, 1993. Wyoming State Archives.

Taylor, Paula Bauman. *F.E. Warren Air Force Base.* Charleston, SC: Arcadia Publishing, 2012.

Thompson, Antonio. *Men in German Uniform: POWs in America during World War II.* Knoxville: University of Tennessee Press, 2010.

U.S. War Department. "P.O.W. Branch Camp, Dubois, Wyo., Site Plan, June 27, 1945." Office of the Post Engineer, Scottsbluff, Nebraska.

———. P.O.W. Branch Camp, Dubois, Wyo. Site Plans. "POW Kitchen and Mess Hall, June 29, 1945." "E.M. Kitchen and Mess Hall, June 30, 1945." "Washrooms, Latrines, Tool Shed and Root Cellar, July 2, 1945." Office of Post Engineer, Scottsbluff, Nebraska.

———. "Prisoner of War Camp Labor Report." Camp Dubois, Wyoming, 1944–1946. Office of the Provost Marshal General. National Archives.

Wind Pudding and Rabbit Tracks: A History of Goshen County, Wyoming. Torrington, WY: Goshen County History Book Committee, 1993.

Wyoming State Park, Historic Sites and Trails. *Camp Douglas Officers' Club State Historic Site.* Undated.

YMCA Reports. Harold Hong. "Report on Visit to Prisoner of War Branch Camp (Scottsbluff), Veteran, Wyoming." December 18, 1944. Scottsbluff, Nebraska files. National Archives.

INDEX

ABOUT THE AUTHOR

Cheryl O'Brien grew up in the Hudson Valley in New York State and enjoyed a career with the New York State Department of Environmental Conservation before relocating to Wyoming in 2002. O'Brien graduated from the University of Wyoming with a BA in social sciences with an emphasis in history and archaeology. Her article "Camp Dubois, Wyoming: A Legacy of Literature" was published in the *Annals of Wyoming: Wyoming History Journal* in fall 2015.

O'Brien lives in Dubois, Wyoming, with her husband, Bill. She often looks up at the mountains from her home where the former Dubois POW camp was located and thinks about the challenges the camp residents faced at the very isolated timber camp.

Visit us at
www.historypress.com